Without Terminus

ALSO BY CHAUN WEBSTER

Wail Song: or wading in the water at the end of the world

Gentry!fication: or the scene of the crime

ADVANCE PRAISE FOR *WITHOUT TERMINUS*

"*Without Terminus* does the uncanny, and absolutely sincere, work of obliterating everything I thought I knew about fracture, memory, labor, and Blackness. chaun webster has created a sturdy, yet dizzying archive and offering that nudges us to critique the ways Black memory and Black labor and Black love of memory and labor are circulated, and ultimately meditated on. The book is as fine, as delightful, as serious as any book I've read this century. There is a staggering gumption at work here, and it is indeed generative and wholly loving of what came before it." **—Kiese Laymon, author of *Heavy***

"The aleatory trane or train or chain chaun webster takes, by which he is foregiven, along which he descends in aeronautical digging, is familial and radically unfamiliar. Old and new, on time, untimely; ungendered, ante-generic, intergenerational; a syntax of busted blocks in a sine wave of irregular collision; a counterpoint of contronyms on corners; a picture book come out itself of portraiture gone past itself. So that what we have here in our hands is as beautiful and bruised and black and blue and bounteous and unbound as we ℝ."

—Fred Moten, author of *Perennial Fashion*

"*Without Terminus* tracks chaun webster gone further into that which won't stop, even for that last, bleak station. In his newest work, the poet considers the possibility of Black rest without Black death, the labor that memory demands of the living, and Black life as both fuel and lubricant for the US progress engine. This work demands of webster new grammars, a hauntology, a means of being without, which is to say a praxis of knowing with grief even that which you can barely mourn. Deeply intimate and tirelessly self-interrogating, *Without Terminus* is webster at his best. Phenomenal!" **—Douglas Kearney, author of *I Imagine I Been Science Fiction Always*** "chaun webster's *Without Terminus* is a beautifully lyrical rumination on unknowing. The word 'terminus' could be the end of a transportation line as well as a finishing point. Right away with the title, we see webster's facility with metaphoric language. For webster, 'without terminus' doesn't mean forever, as in elongated emptiness, but 'frayed edges' as a reclamation and new space, the limits as haven. This book is a marvel, a language and image train to travel with." **—Victoria Chang, author of *With My Back to the World***

"chaun webster does not write easy books. *Without Terminus* is an unflinching document of familial love and the legacy of Blackness in America. It is an act of revolution cloaked in the language of poetry, wielding a heart full of courage."
—Kao Kalia Yang, author of *Where Rivers Part*

"webster, already a formidable poet, charts a genealogy of loss through an inquiry and lyric form of his own making, gifting a map that cracks open the expansive possibilities of memoir. . . . webster wonders 'if blackness is the grammar of loss in the modern world' and if 'we have all been had, gotten over, by the archive and the slippery words that make blackness known only when it is *about to disappear*.' Perhaps yes, but *Without Terminus* ardently contends with these erasures of the Black past, present, and future." **—Lillian-Yvonne Bertram, author of *Negative Money***

Without Terminus

untraining an archive

CHAUN WEBSTER

Graywolf Press

Published by Graywolf Press
212 Third Avenue North, Suite 485
Minneapolis, Minnesota 55401

www.graywolfpress.org

Published in the United States of America

ISBN 978-1-64445-392-6 (paperback)
ISBN 978-1-64445-393-3 (ebook)

2 4 6 8 9 7 5 3 1
First Graywolf Printing, 2026

Library of Congress Cataloging-in-Publication Data

Names: Webster, Chaun author
Title: Without terminus : untraining an archive / Chaun Webster.
Description: Minneapolis, Minnesota : Graywolf Press, 2026. | Includes bibliographical references.
Identifiers: LCCN 2025048771 (print) | LCCN 2025048772 (ebook) | ISBN 9781644453926 trade paperback | ISBN 9781644453933 epub
Subjects: LCGFT: Creative nonfiction
Classification: LCC PS3623.E39575 W58 2026 (print) | LCC PS3623.E39575 (ebook)
LC record available at https://lccn.loc.gov/2025048771
LC ebook record available at https://lccn.loc.gov/2025048772

Cover design: Crisis

Cover photos: Dorothea Lange, *Untitled*, 1939, from the Library of Congress, Prints & Photographs Division, Farm Security Administration / Office of War Information Black-and-White Negatives (train); Creative Commons CC0 1.0 Universal Public Domain (Minneapolis Third Precinct, May 28, 2020)

for my here gone,
& my gone gone

without

chaun

terminus

webster

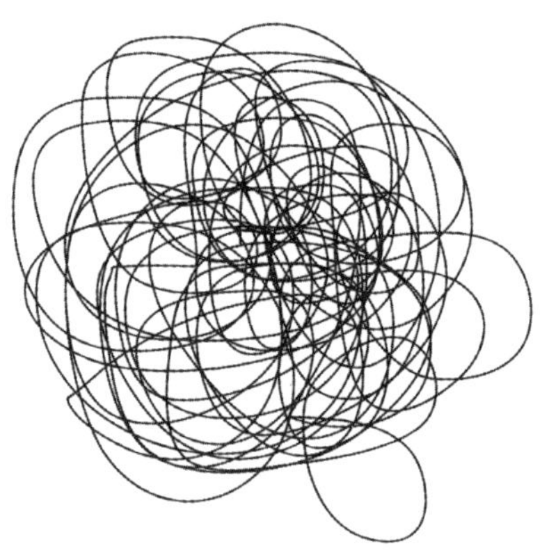

I start in the middle of the sentence and
move both directions at once.

—John Coltrane

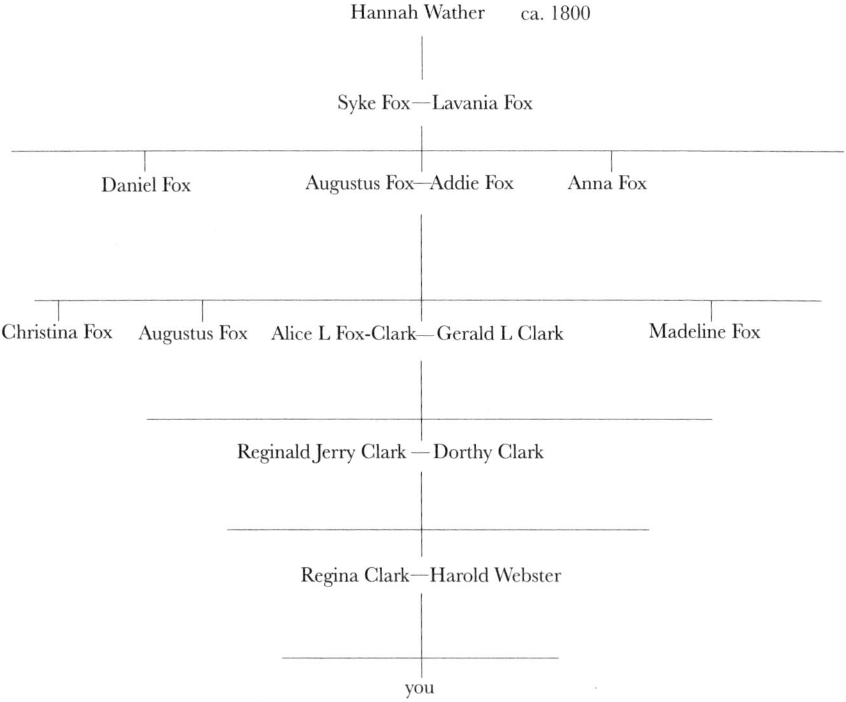

Hannah Wather ca. 1800

Syke Fox—Lavania Fox

Daniel Fox Augustus Fox—Addie Fox Anna Fox

Christina Fox Augustus Fox Alice L Fox-Clark—Gerald L Clark Madeline Fox

Reginald Jerry Clark —Dorthy Clark

Regina Clark—Harold Webster

you

1 *your grandfather worked twenty-five years as a porter for the Great Northern Railroad and when he retired all they gave him was a pen with the number twenty-five on it.*

my mother ended this sentence. she moved on to another while i studied each word from this one, rotating them to assess their dimension and weight, looking underneath the vocabulary's shape to capture its shadows. the comma is a graphic gesture outside of language but not outside of meaning. its curvature a half moon extending the idea in a sentence, stretching its thought, and making space for breath. there have been many sentences that have found their way to me lacking this curved marker, their whispered abruptness a violence. my mother's sentence needed a comma, needed a bit more breath.

2 i am the grandchild and great grandchild of rail workers. both of them porters of the sleeping car, both of them having demands placed upon their bodies that interdicted their rest. during their employment they were both suspended in the irony of the sleeping car, which stole their ability to sleep, that robbery of rest a down payment for the ease of white train passengers. it is a familiar formula. i am trying to extend the sentences that arrived to me from my mother, and later the railroad's archive, extend them into a different kind of exhaustion and limit point, to see where their lines fracture and whether i can step into the space made by their splitting. i am attempting to insert the curvature of the comma into the sentence and line, a speculative practice emerging from a desire to converse with ghosts.

3 in high school my English teachers would tell me that my writing had too many commas, that the rules of grammar did not afford the fifteen i was attempting to smuggle into a single sentence. they would tell me *be concise, get to the point*, and round and round i kept going. and while i do not resist the concise in every instance, there is something about the black rhetorical tradition that calls on the sentence to go a little further, that utilizes the comma in order to insert breath in it, it is the whoop of the black sermon, where the breath is pause comma and emphasis comma and melody.

Ashon Crawley writes about a sermon given by Juandolyn Stokes where the *texture of sound created through the inhalation and exhalation of interaction of air with flesh* creates an opening in the collective breathing and enunciation of the church. *her whooping produced the sonic space as discontinuous and open, open to other voices that proceeded her moment of being overcome with Spirit.* OOOOOOOOOh Ahhhhh, my my laaawd, give us commas dear lawd sweaty as the arched backs that labored all week to bring us before the altar, give us breath whooping, OOOOOOOOh laaaaaawd OOOOOOOOOOh my my laaaaaawd against the weapons formed against me, against the routine suppression of black breathing, our breathing an insistence outside the sentence's capacity to hold or to apprehend.

4 i return frequently to the threshing floor scene of James Baldwin's *Go Tell It on the Mountain*. in it, the main character, John Grimes, while at the threshing floor of his storefront church, goes down down to a space *swallowed up in chaos* down down where *darkness does not present a point of departure, contains no beginning, and no end*, and it is there in the *no beginning, and no end* of that darkness that Grimes meets god, is overtaken by the holy ghost, *was wordless*. and it is in the *world-*

less doubt and darkness, itself a kind of hermeneutic, that Grimes experiences revelation. each time i read this scene there is something that changes in the tenor of my voice and in the tempo of my reading. i hear the organ building as Grimes tries to *see through the morning wall* and *tear the thousand gray veils of the sky away* and i am breathing as i would be were i delivering a sermon, each comma in Baldwin's impossibly long sentences taking me down down into the darkness of blackness with Grimes, my knees knelt at the threshing floor with him as i am wordless and in revelation in the company of my ghosts.

5 i have been writing letters to my dead. i have several that i have written to my great grandmother Alice, someone i've never met and yet miss, a strange affectual pull i have been responding to by writing her. in the letter there is the salutation, the comma, and what comes after. the birth and the afterbirth of the letter.

i feel easily frustrated by the orthographic reduction in the salutation. how, when i haven't spoken to a loved one in a while, there is more affective pressure in my greeting, my hello carries my heartache and elation, it holds an advance communication of my longing to communicate. *Dear Alice,* says more than the symbols alone can convey in this mediated set of relations with my dead. how to not become formulaic, how to not allow the letter to be only the body, the afterbirth that follows the comma.

i have been burying my letters to Alice, pouring water over the soil that covers them. i have been trying to imagine a response, something on both sides of a comma that is more than the sayable.

6 the furthest back i can reach in my maternal grandfather's line is to Hannah Wather. it is a line that is less line than fractal, more fracture than genealogical foundation, a train from which i seem to always be departing and never arriving.

i arrive at Hannah through a database search in a federal census record shrouded in language of place, and position, and labor. abrupt sentences i am trying to extend. Hannah Wather: at home. Hannah Wather: keeper of the house. Hannah Wather: black female, eighty years old. Hannah Wather with no precise record of birth or death. Hannah Wather, gone.

7 what does it mean to be gone? or to have so much difficulty in proving the here-ness of my kin? when history has arrived to me fractured already my instinct is to engage in a recovery mission. but i am unsure if this is one.

8 i am preoccupied with absence, with what has been absented. the stolen names of ancestors, the crafty ways terror hides under the vocabulary of *acquire* or *progress*, *discover* or *wage*, how we can absent the appearance of a word's teeth while they are sinking into our flesh. but i also know absence to be an artistic material, the chasm between two words in the poetic line, what the cavern of the negative space has the potential to hold. these gestures of bodily and linguistic absence and excess were a part of my upbringing as a black pentecostal. there are familiar moments when the pastor would be slowly saying something about *the midnight hour* and *night won't last always*, the organist playing beneath and alongside these articulations, both building in intensity

as congregants are shouting, humming, swaying, as someone bends their body, their curved back shape-shifting into a comma, removing their heels and yielding to the holy ghost, racing round the congregation in ecstatic worship. returning to these memories i discern a poetics in the movement, in the multiform gestures that exceed language. i am still trying to write them, and failing.

9 Renee Gladman has been rewiring how i think about prose. the drawings that she makes with abstract lines are writing, Gladman calls them *Prose Architectures*, and the sentences she writes are also drawings. some of Gladman's prose architectures are tall structures i would feel terrified to climb while others are whole cities or a narrow row of houses. all of these prose architectures in one way or another compel me to imagine placing my body inside of them, walking their streets, entering their rooms. in Gladman's *One Long Black Sentence*, she takes another turn into prose, and while on one register the title produces a frightening connection to the carceral, where a sentence's length is simultaneously a way a life is shortened, on another register this long black sentence of Gladman's does something outside enclosure, Gladman's single black sentence, which is many drawings, spans a space that is not enclosed by the period, goes on, pauses, and then goes on again. not so much a long sentence as a kind of longing. in *Plans for Sentences* Gladman highlights a break from the enclosure i believe rhymes with the ongoingness of her long and longing sentence, saying:

These sentences will gather all the pauses into a flowing assembly, into a speech that is only the comma, and will hold time as it distills and blackens in equation it is the pauses that are being gathered by the sentences, and yet this gathering of pauses is flowing, they are suspending and inaugurating motion, they are holding and perhaps attempting to swallow time. and here again, the carceral, in that the metrics of punishment for those who are sentenced is time, but time here is being held by and distilled through the black hands that are writing the pausing-flowing sentences, and so again, maybe there is an equation that is being reached for through a sentence that we refuse to end and as a result of our holding it, also intend to outlast.

10 the line i have been tracing and attempting to extend through Regina and Harold, Reginald and Dorthy, Jerry and Alice, Augustus and Addie, Lavania and Syke, this line i have been writing alongside and under has led me to Hannah, a palindrome, a name on the other side of a sentence i have begun in the middle of.

Hannah is recorded to be near eighty years old on an 1880 federal census. mother to Syke Fox, grandmother to Anna, Augustus, and Daniel. Fox, a surname that begins with Syke in the record, and with no explanation, but follows through Augustus and Addie, on to Alice Fox who would become a Clark. Alice, my great grandmother and Reginald's mother. Hannah, my four times great grandmother. i can see no further than Hannah. i can only see Hannah dimly. i cannot help but fill in the gaps, fabulating from the elisions.

perhaps Wather was the surname of some family who believed they owned my four times great grandmother. a propertied logic underwritten with profound violence. maybe one night as she sits by a fire, heavy from her years, from all the sentences that have accrued within them, Hannah tells her child some of the details of what underwote the propertied logic of the Wathers, slipping unaware into the telling like walking backward into her own name, a strange combination of words describing something and someone unfamiliar. Syke then may have decided in the slow boil of impossible black life that they loved Hannah and themself more than the name by which they were known, that there were other ways to know themselves. and so, Syke too walks backward into another grammar, something like a fox using the earth's magnetic field for precision. an imaginative gesture where Syke understood that the self, the person, were always already fictions that drew aberrant borders they were always outside of. that they could choose other fictions, other selves, or no selves at all, intent on holding what others sought to harm. intent on refusing consent to the very terms of that order. this other becoming, one without an arrival and on the edge of its own undoing, is the point.

11 write a line, extend it, pause, stretch
it out, again, make it go,
further write a pause, stretch
it out, go make it out, go, go, again,

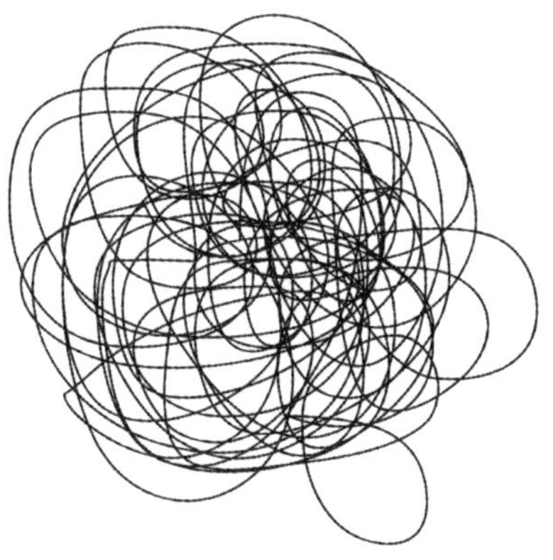

How does one narrate the loss of loss?

—Frank Wilderson

They will say that I am unkillable, that my body resists battery by tree trunks, bullets, and years in small cells.

—Dawn Lundy Martin

tell us a story . . .

of the righteousness of work, the never-too-muchness of its pressures. there are so many seductive versions of its myths. the ballad of John Henry has hundreds of variations. a prototypical american story of labor. the story goes that at the emergence of the steam-powered drill, which eventually would replace the backs and hands and arms that swung hammers to drive steel through solid rock in the building of train tracks, John Henry challenges this machine to a race. the story goes that John Henry, with his heroic strength, races the machine drilling and drilling again in repetitive motion, drilling past desire, past his own body's fatigue, until there is little distinction between his body and the hammer, his hammer body seizing victory from automation. and at the end of that legendary race, the story goes that John Henry uses his last words to ask for a cool drink of water. some accounts have him drinking it while others don't say, but in every version John Henry's heart gives out from the strain of it all. he collapses, dying from exhaustion with his hammer in hand.

often this story is told to highlight black resilience or the might of the human will over technology, to say that our bodies will keep going, beyond the untiring machines, our bodies are machines themselves that forgo rest and do not need relief. but this ballad is blues, and in the triumphant telling, John Henry's body and strength are reduced to labor and hammer and whatever righteousness is registered in them, and as he—body racked—somehow makes out a request for that cool drink of water, one he may have never brought to his parched lips, he finds that neither water nor resilience nor strength could stop the premature dying. his body retired.

your mother tells you a story about retirement, your grandfather's twenty-five years of service as a pullman porter. every time you say the title you feel the word *pull* stretching itself out in your mouth, a pullllllllman porter. she told you of the constraints of his labor, its years, and how they pulled from him, pulled years from him, how he would retire without pension and then would die with no triumphant ballad. your mother is the inaugural archive, your point of origin for what you come to know about your grandfather, *archive* here being a slippery word. one that could indicate a physical geography where the collected materials of history have been stored or something more ephemeral, a body of knowledge, the archive of maternal experience. both are full of elisions and gaps, you step into them.

T-73A(06-84) 6,52(

RAILROAD RETIREMENT NOTICE

RAILROAD RETIREMENT NOTICE

a mass of stories get imposed on experience, on the archive, comporting its materials to its shape, becoming the lens by which not only the events and sequence of the past are determined but also their meaning. you are a student of story. a familiar one is that of uplift through adversity. that those who work and toil do so with the eventuality of ascendancy. another ballad of John Henry. as a black child you are told this until it becomes elemental to how you interpret the world: work, child, you must work, you must work harder, twice as hard as your white counterpart. as though there is something transformative in the labor, the sweat of your brow a baptism into some meritocratic family of god. your grandfather Reginald would work long hours in tight quarters. a pullman porter. George Pullman, designer of the Pullman Palace Car, which later became the sleeping car, would capitalize on this story of uplift, drawing the majority of his service personnel from the formerly enslaved. work, you must work, and then ascend. all you need do is serve, all you need do is step into the role of the nameless worker, the boy or the George. all you need do is comport the too-largeness of your presence into a familiar racial architecture, a story of workers willing to swallow a thousand indignities with a smile, willing to devour their own heart meat over miles of track so that others might rest.

by the time your grandfather was working as a porter, the Pullman Company was the largest employer of black folks in the united states. and if the train functioned as a fantasy of american progress, the porter functioned as a fantasy of inexhaustible black labor, a remnant of a pastoral time.

NAME OF EM-
PLOYEE OR
ENROLLEE(1ST
INITIAL AND 5
LETTERS OF
LAST)
37-42

R *
CLARK

you had a maternal grandfather. Reginald Jerry Clark. dead eight years and a day prior to your birth. read backward you were a grandchild to a Clark, who is gone, was dead. he is a porter for the Great Northern Railroad, was working in compressed space. his hours are not his own.

stories are full of characters, like the wise man or woman who is missing an eye, or the long-suffering protagonist, or the fool. these types are bones that structure a character's potential. you are not immune from drawing them. in fact, saying some names feels as though you are sketching a character, always incomplete. the messy lines being drawn inevitably crack, pasts leaking from their fissures. what are the rules of imagining kin, of calling your gone as though they are more than once bodies, than bare life? what does it mean when the train and miles of track, when steam and coal and freight car are all notations on the character, written over them like a second skin?

to *com port* as intransitive verb is to be fitting, often in terms of behavior: the porter *comports* to the directive. its prefix com-*with*, the Latin word *comportare* meant *to bring together*. coincide, cohere, correspond, rhyme. and what is forcibly being brought together by language? what happens when the body is inconsistent with the container it is violently being required to correspond with? when it will not comport, a word that sounds to you like com-porter, that you easily confuse with compartment, where you store something away, cordon it off—what happens when your being does not rhyme with the world? is it the line or you yourself that must be broken?

you cannot bring together the complex material of your grandfather's life through story, something is always erased from the surface when you attempt to constrict the dimensions of his living with that of a scene or chapter that takes place in the forty-two-inch-by-twenty-five-inch sleeping car and is reproduced on this five-and-a-half-by-eight-and-a-quarter page. even the one hundred twenty pages from Reginald's employment files, which you have purchased photocopies of from the National Archives in Atlanta, are compressed, comport less to a life than to its abbreviation.

Harriet Jacobs knew something about comportment, about bending her body in tight space to remain hidden. Jacobs, who was enslaved, which is in part to say subjected to another's story, would evade her captors by spending seven years in her grandmother's garret in Edenton, North Carolina, nine feet by seven feet by three feet at its tallest. compression. it would do irreparable damage to her body, but within the spectrum of her choices, if we are to call them choices, this is a damage she found more tolerable than slavery. she would call it a *loophole of retreat*. where can you retreat from the loss, or from the geography of the taking? Jacobs chooses the garret, she does not desire it. it was a gamble she would make against her body, that her body could outlast the horror outside her nine feet by seven feet by three feet cell. the body sometimes being the only site from which to make a wager and that wager being what we believe the body can withstand. as she wrote *Incidents in the Life of a Slave Girl*, her ex-slave narrative, her body undoubtedly still echoed with the pain from her confinement in the garret. to stay did wreckage to the body and to leave only meant reentry into another network of violence. you are concerned about valorizing the garret, about imposing ascendancy.

even as Jacobs wrote on the *loophole of retreat*, she was likely wincing.

Reginald would name your mother Regina, his fourth and last daughter. you wonder if he was waiting expectantly for a boy child given the gendered relationship to namesakes and what is passed on. you wonder if your mother ever felt she needed to squeeze herself within the skeleton of his name, comporting to expectations that preceded either of them, expectations that clashed with her body.

Regina tells you Reginald was a gambler, believes in the probability of something other than a few coins in his pocket. that he would tell your grandmother to always bet on seven and eleven. indivisible numbers. he was reckless with money. there was a day when they had no food. there were many days like this, when the hunger occupied more space than the means to assuage it. on one such day Reginald would leave the house with less than it would take to feed your mother, her three sisters, your grandmother. he would return with a bag of groceries, tomatoes and beans, rice and chicken. it was not said, but everyone knew. seven and eleven. he was subject to hours of labor for which he was not paid, a wage that required tips to live. this is not called theft. there is a way work can grind against the bones, the cells, a way that it stretches the skin, hardens it, makes the body something closer to a machine. not the train, not unlike the train. there are more hours than are counted, than can be counted. this too is a wager, one made upon Reginald's body. one Reginald made with his body. like so many breaths, so many heartbeats. one way of measuring time in a life. in looking over Reginald's medical records you see the visits to the hospital in the years leading up to his death, his complaint of chest pains, a tight compression in his body, a shortness of breath, the doctors telling him that nothing was abnormal, the eventual failure of his heart. how many times would it pulse before reaching terminus?

when you are old enough Regina will tell you that you are magic, born on the seventh day of the eleventh month, almost as though you were a prayer sent up against stakes he was not meant to survive. he has left your mother his wallet, a ring, and a pen. she believes they were meant for you after he dies on the eighth day of the eleventh month, eight years before you are born. a numbers game she uses to explain the rotten fortune, a numbers game you know you'll lose, are losing. innumerable bets placed on a future you still have no grammar for, a future casting a shadow. the ring was a material marker of employment for the Great Northern Railroad. costly, precious. given greater care than the body that wore it. the ring making the shape of a zero, from the Arabic *sifr*, meaning empty, shape-shifting into the Italian, *zefiro*, and later the English, *zero*. *zefiro*, meaning west wind. sometimes you imagine the shape of nothing, of emptiness, not the round symbol of the ring, but a body, one without a name. the ring would be stolen from the apartment you lived in as a child, the robbery a loss indistinguishable from so many others. sometimes you try to imagine yourself capable of summoning the west wind, *zefiro*, a substitute inheritance that gives shape to the emptiness.

in 1849 Henry Box Brown, who at the time was enslaved, paid eighty-six dollars to mail himself to Philadelphia, Pennsylvania, from Richmond, Virginia, in a wooden crate. his body held years of compressed weight in a box three feet long by two feet wide and two feet deep. contraband. not unlike the three hundred black migrants working their way up the Mississippi by steamboat in 1868 detained at Fort Snelling as contraband of war. the movement of black bodies conscripted to always be fugitive. Brown smuggles himself aboard the Adams Express Company in a box as railroad freight. freight, or goods transported in bulk by train or to be burdened as one who is freighted with too much history. Brown enters the box, itself a kind of tomb lined with a cloth, having but a small hole for air, and labeled dry goods. compressed for twenty-seven hours, making his body small, and smaller, constricting his breath in the darkness of enclosure. he would emerge in reenactments of his stealing away by postage as though being resurrected from the dead. Lazarus still wearing his burial clothes. Henry, a magician knowing the art of escape, of concealing his body, more water than anything, as dry goods on a freight train.

a black geography is confined space. the hold of the ship, the tight dimensions of a *loophole of retreat*. blackness becomes a shorthand for confinement, the principal image of carcerality, and even to loosen the shackle you need to enter the box, to become freight. and aboard the train, a porter, traveling in the sleeping car, on the rare occasion of rest would do so in the baggage room, stored among so many dried goods.

you wonder if your grandfather stepped aboard the train's sleeping car as if working his way into a garret, as though climbing into a box. a box where the constriction of space functions by disallowing its luxuries to the porter. not even the space the porter occupies is their own. you wonder if Reginald believed he would outlast the banal accumulation of days under this regime of nonspace. did he put his trust in retirement, which is a story about work, a story about how work over a period of twenty or thirty years can be transformed into rest? you have a photo of Reginald stepping off the train, arms slack beside him, staring ahead at someone with a technology that affixes his body to time even as the train puts him in motion. you know too much of the story, like the black characters you see in film or read about whose ruin serves as narrative propulsion, fuel to keep the vehicle going, you know how it ends, but this doesn't stop you from desiring another outcome, to climb into the borders of an inverted photograph like Henry's box and whisper a secret or two about what's around the bend.

E

a black rail worker was born in 1913, served as a porter for the Great Northern Railroad for twenty-five years, and then retired; he died some time later. in 1913 there was a rail worker, a porter. he served the Great Northern Railroad and died some time after retirement. a rail worker served as a porter and then retired. for twenty-five years, a porter served the Great Northern Railroad. he was born in 1913, he was black, he died. a rail worker was a porter for twenty-five years, he worked for retirement, he died. a rail worker died after retirement. a black was born a rail worker, a porter for the Great Northern. he served, he retired. a black worker was born a porter for the railroad and retirement was later, later. a black worker died, he retired later. for twenty-five years, a rail worker died for the Great Northern Railroad. retirement was always after. a black serves, and rails and dies on the road some time later he is born a porter. a black was born a railroad, was born dying. twenty-five years is some time, black is retired time, the later born still serve. if a black is born on the railroad after twenty-five years, he dies and the Great Northern says he served and retired. if a black doesn't work, he dies on the railroad. if a black works for the railroad, he dies a Great Northern death. in 1913 some say blacks are born porters serving Great Northern fantasies of retirement. a rail worker laughs later and dies. some say progress is born with the rail, twenty-five years later a porter cannot serve, cannot retire, and so he dies. black years are born working on some railroad of the great north, the train moves, black years are still. a rail worker cannot retire, so he dies and haunts the railroad. a railroad cannot be born unless a black dies, but such is progress. somewhere along the railroad there is a group of blacks building a coffin waiting to be born porters. something about the great north requires a black porter dying to retire but who ends up only dying. something about the railroad shores up an imagined forward. it does so by steamrolling through black rail workers. they all die and cannot retire. when a black is born may the ledger show accounts are payable to the railroad. if you do not have a black worker, imagine the railroad and service and the sound of their dying. now you may lie down and retire. some say later we all retire on some big railroad up in the great north beyond, the blacks are dying to find out. heard that the railroad was a jolly ride, that twenty-five years was a blink the great north tickling every imaginable fancy to the tune of blacks dying. some say a train awaits to abduct the black born, their years a wraith. if you should find yourself a black worker for some railroad of the north, twenty-five years of dying will prove insufficient for retirement. blacks born dead on the rail rail and wail, but they never retire.

did he make it out alive? you already know the answer to this question, yet you are still compelled to ask. you work with words, which unlike the empty wallet you have inherited is not a material you can touch, but you wonder if in reordering this material you might disrupt what is presupposed. but no new order has ever changed the outcome.

in 1969 Reginald would have an acute coronary occlusion. blood flow to his heart was blocked from a buildup of plaque that can accrue from diet or smoking or stress. it would be the first in a series of occlusions that occur before eventual heart failure. there is no cause of death that will say the strain of work or lack of sleep or comporting oneself to the specifications of nonpersonhood were what resulted in the failure of Reginald's heart, the tightness in his chest from the blockage in his arteries a visual parallel to tracks, not being resolvable by compression or by sending electrical shocks to restore the rhthym of his vital organ. after seven more years of circumnavigating how to perform presence and absence coterminously, a hollowed-out receptacle, his strained heart will stop, and death will be compressed into a date and the name of the deceased and the city in which the death occurred. evidence. a story told in the restricted syntactical arrangement of the medical document. this is a box that cannot be mailed to freedom. your grandfather was freight, is fraught, and not free.

DISCHARGE SUMMARY

[illegible] Fatigue — Breathing
With chest pain — Heart rate
[illegible] July 15th 1976
She came into hospital
of persistent heart chest pain
[illegible]
tinued to have heart chest pa

EATH

E OF DECEASED AS SHOWN ON EVIDENCE: Reginald J. Clark

23 DATE OF DEATH: 11 08 76

CE OF DEATH (CITY AND STATE): St. Paul Mn

25 KIND OF DOCUMENT: [X] DEATH CERTIFICATE

NSTRUCTIONS FOR COMPLETING THIS FORM:

lete all items applicable to the proofs being established. The date of birth and the date of the document must s be completed for each proof of age. If only the age is shown on the document, enter the age and the date of established by the document. If the date of the document is not shown, enter the last day of the year estimated the date the record was recorded. Also, compute the weight of the document by adding the type value (Item 20) age value (Item 21) and enter the total weight value in Items 6(e), 7(e) or 8(e), depending on whose birth date ing established. If multiple documents are being transcribed for two or three persons, show a symbol after pe and the age of the document as follows:

APPLICANT	SYMBOL	APPLICANT	SYMBOL
MPLOYEE	E	WIDOW (WIDOWER)	W
POUSE	S	CHILD	C

delayed birth registration the weight and date of record should be based on the oldest acceptable evidence to obtain the delayed birth registration. See the Field Operating Manual or the Retirement Claims Manual aluation of proofs.

your mother tells you Reginald *worked for twenty-five years as a porter and when he retired all they gave him was a pen with the number twenty-five on it*. this was the story you were told. but while sitting with the abbreviated files of your grandfather—one way the railroad arranges and constricts a story of work—you notice a check he was sent by the railroad retirement board in the amount of $573. it is a record of Reginald receiving a pension, perhaps the only payment. it is dated a month after he died. the dead cannot cash checks. there is a return date marked for the thirteenth of December. you imagine the impact this must have had on your grandmother, to receive this check after Reginald's death and be made to return it. his body not long in the ground and the railroad still demanding something of him. this check, a poor notation of hours over years under which his body is the principal currency for the luxury white passengers of the sleeping car consume. Reginald's story exceeds the check, which you have requested more than the photocopy of and been denied. you are told that the National Archives in Atlanta does not own this record, they only steward it for the railroad retirement board. the railroad owned the labor, they own the evidence of it. the archive dispossessing you of both. you keep bringing the photocopied materials together, knowing they will always be a too-narrow container, what you are wanting surpasses storied description.

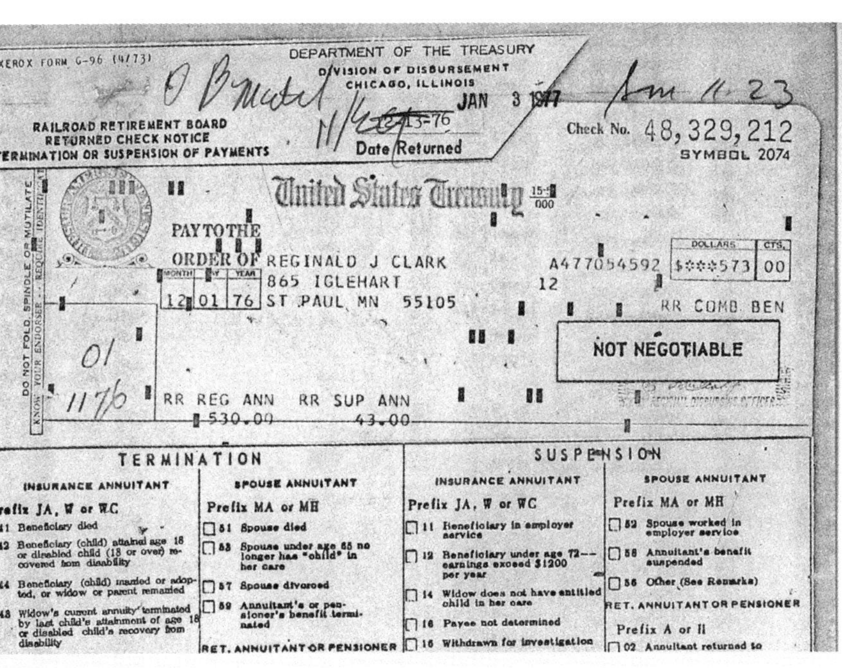

XEROX FORM G-96 (4/73)

DEPARTMENT OF THE TREASURY
DIVISION OF DISBURSEMENT
CHICAGO, ILLINOIS

JAN 3 1977

RAILROAD RETIREMENT BOARD
RETURNED CHECK NOTICE
TERMINATION OR SUSPENSION OF PAYMENTS

12-13-76
Date Returned

Check No. 48,329,212
SYMBOL 2074

United States Treasury 15-51/000

PAY TO THE ORDER OF REGINALD J CLARK
865 IGLEHART
ST PAUL MN 55105

MONTH	DAY	YEAR
12	01	76

A477054592 12

DOLLARS	CTS.
$***573	00

RR COMB. BEN

NOT NEGOTIABLE

DO NOT FOLD, SPINDLE OR MUTILATE
KNOW YOUR ENDORSER — REQUIRE IDENTIFICATION

01
11 76

RR REG ANN 530.00 RR SUP ANN 43.00

TERMINATION

INSURANCE ANNUITANT

Prefix JA, W or WC

41 Beneficiary died
42 Beneficiary (child) attained age 18 or disabled child (18 or over) recovered from disability
44 Beneficiary (child) married or adopted, or widow or parent remarried
43 Widow's current annuity terminated by last child's attainment of age 18 or disabled child's recovery from disability

SPOUSE ANNUITANT

Prefix MA or MH

☐ 51 Spouse died
☐ 53 Spouse under age 65 no longer has "child" in her care
☐ 57 Spouse divorced
☐ 59 Annuitant's or pensioner's benefit terminated

RET. ANNUITANT OR PENSIONER

SUSPENSION

INSURANCE ANNUITANT

Prefix JA, W or WC

☐ 11 Beneficiary in employer service
☐ 12 Beneficiary under age 72—earnings exceed $1200 per year
☐ 14 Widow does not have entitled child in her care
☐ 16 Payee not determined
☐ 16 Withdrawn for investigation

SPOUSE ANNUITANT

Prefix MA or MH

☐ 52 Spouse worked in employer service
☐ 58 Annuitant's benefit suspended
☐ 56 Other (See Remarks)

RET. ANNUITANT OR PENSIONER

Prefix A or H

☐ 02 Annuitant returned to

the term *free black*
carries tension
within its structure;
it brings two
disparate grammars
into collusion and
collision
produces ontological
catastrophe

you are exchanging words. *collision* for *collusion*, not of two trains, but *two disparate grammars*, that of freedom and of blackness which structures subjection. your maternal grandfather's body being the site of impact. there is no ground beneath you, beneath the collision. it is as though these two speeding vocabularies—a complex network of nonrelation, a syntactical stage of violence—are moving toward each other midair. you are exchanging words, but no clever contortion you make of them can produce a different cinema from catastrophe. you are still stuck with the wreckage. *you* and *wreckage* here, a redundancy.

tell us a story . . .

nothing written here can bring back the dead or pay a just wage. nothing written here will bring this world to its end. it is only perhaps a prelude to a sharpened blade. scribble away child, we might still skewer something tomorrow.

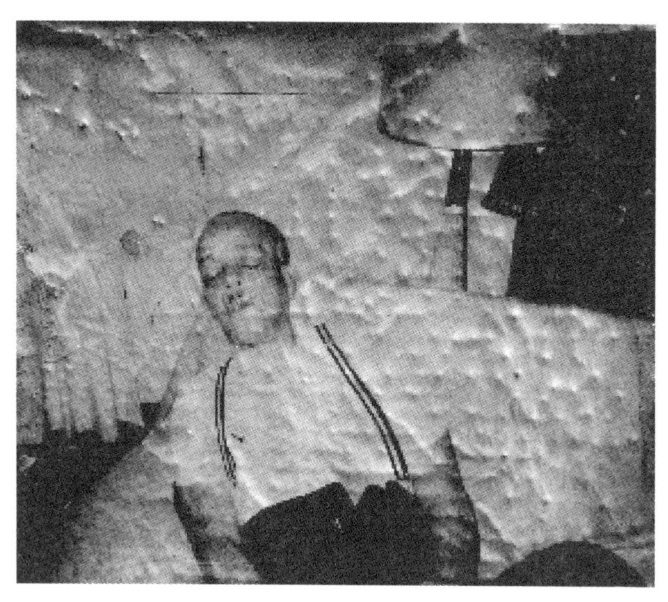

PHOTOGRAPH
REGINALD JERRY CLARK
YEAR UNKNOWN
SAINT PAUL, MN

DREAM SEQUENCE #1

you begin reposed & in the dream. this is not to make an asymmetry between the so-called real and fiction, this is to indicate another territory. folded arms & eyelids, blackest against Hurston's described sharp-whiteness, but this is not the dream. in that territory there is a child standing in a field among the choral pronouncements of innumerable life-forms & then the focus of some other eye taking you further & further out—& then wide—which is when you see it, a rope-like finger of wind & sky touching that field & the child no longer standing, but running toward the storm.

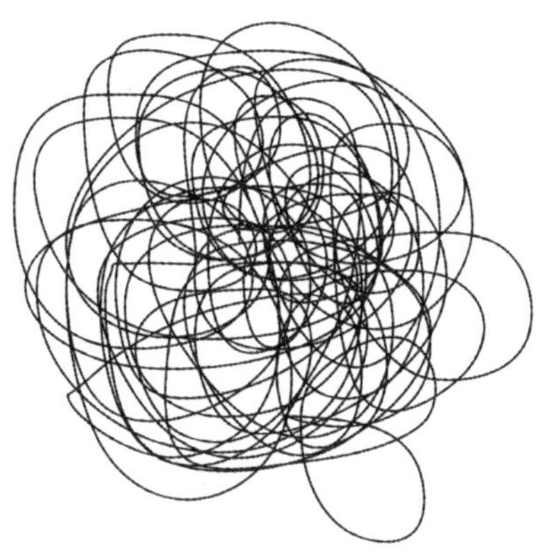

Is there an underground railroad in the sentence?

—Fred Moten

you've been thinking about the sentence as writing that takes place above ground, bringing together the subject and predicate to say something or ask something, certainly to say or ask those things to completion (and here is typically where you would insert a period, concluding the idea and moving on to another) and if this is the protocol of the sentence, can you bring it underground, can you take the sentence and go astray,

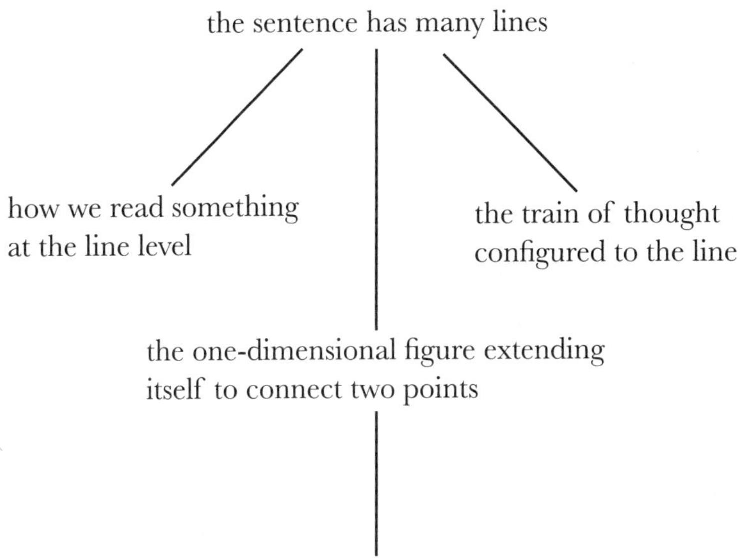

you imagine yourself as one of those points that the sentence or line has led to, in this way the line is spatial and temporal, an arrow or widow's peak pointing toward something; you are unsure if you are the intercept or destination; the sentence you are concerned with appears above the ground of an article, a headline, that reads:

ST. PAUL MAN DIES AFTER ILLNESS OF SHORT DURATION

St. Paul Man Dies After Illness of Short Duration

Mr. Jerry Clark, resident of St. Paul for 25 years, died shortly after becoming ill on a street car on his way to work at the Union depot, where he has been employed for some time as a red cap. He was removed from the street car and taken to Ancker Hospital, where he died an hour later. Mr. Clark was well known throughout the Twin Cities and had many friends.

The cause of his sudden death has not been determined.

your great grandfather worked the train line as a porter also, he would become ill on a streetcar on his way to work, it is the beginning of a sentence, preceded by the subject in the headline ST. PAUL MAN DIES AFTER ILLNESS OF SHORT DURATION and here you are also thinking about the duration of the sentence alongside that of Jerry's illness; he is sentenced, and sentencing the guilty is a means of adding a number of days or months or years in which the body is restricted, it is time both added to and subtracted from the body, so Jerry is here sentenced to the train line, is on his way and on a streetcar from which his body need be removed, that removal followed by another: *he died an hour later, the cause of his sudden death has not been determined*; but what is the sentence but a determination of the body's removal, nothing subtle or sudden, it is the ongoing removal of the ~~black body~~ from the line, a sentence proceeding to its punctuated end:

ST. PAUL MAN DIES AFTER ILLNESS

postscript of

personhood

or appeal for it

such as: I AM A MAN

am dying

to become one

an abbreviation
of saint—
some robed, some holy,
some revered,
but almost always dead—
your dead are not saints
your dead are abbreviated

what is
the after
in the
always already

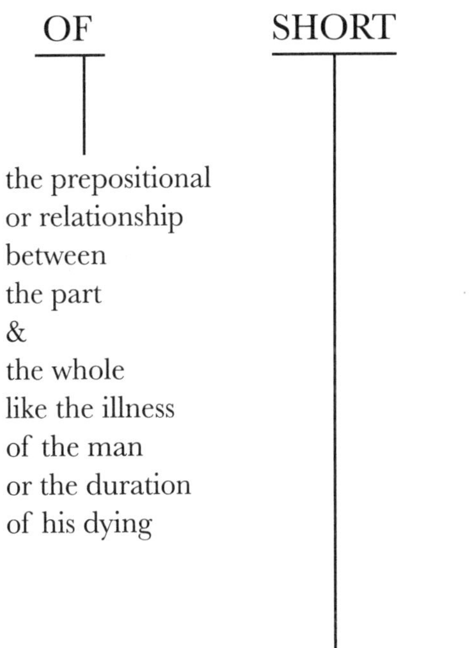

OF SHORT DURATION

the prepositional
or relationship
between
the part
&
the whole
like the illness
of the man
or the duration
of his dying

the time during which
the illness or the dying
or the after the time
during which the man;
the time of illness of
St., of the short after;
the time during which
man dies, where ill-
ness shorts man of an
after; the St. Paul man
dies not of illness, the
St. Paul man dies of
duration

epigram collapsing on a streetcar—short time
abutted by a long sentence—

ST. PAUL MAKES YOU WONDER ABOUT THE DRAW

how time
spills from
the body
collides
with it
makes of the
body
a city's
remains

a clock, each hand an
attempt at a kind of
precision for
time's owners
draw a streetcar
a redcap
draw the body
that wears it
draw the worn body's
exhaustion
& as you accumulate
an image through
tentative lines
draw the line
that ain't one

for an escape
at first
but sundown
is everywhere
in america

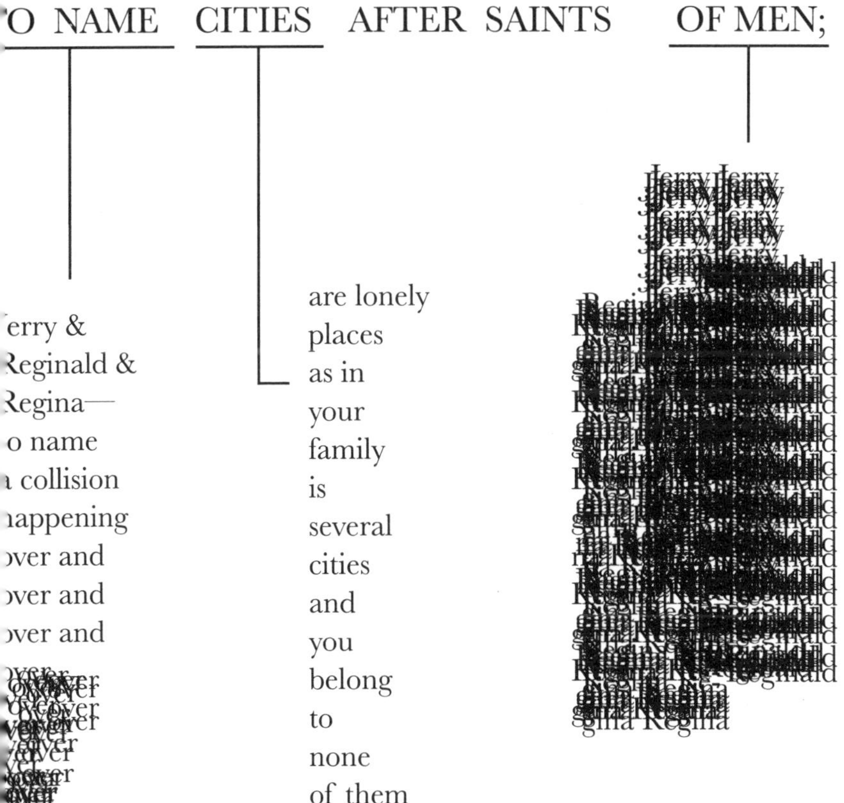

O NAME
CITIES
AFTER
SAINTS
OF MEN;
erry &
eginald &
egina—
o name
collision
appening
ver and
ver and
ver and
are lonely
places
as in
your
family
is
several
cities
and
you
belong
to
none
of them
Jerry Jerry
Reginald
Regina

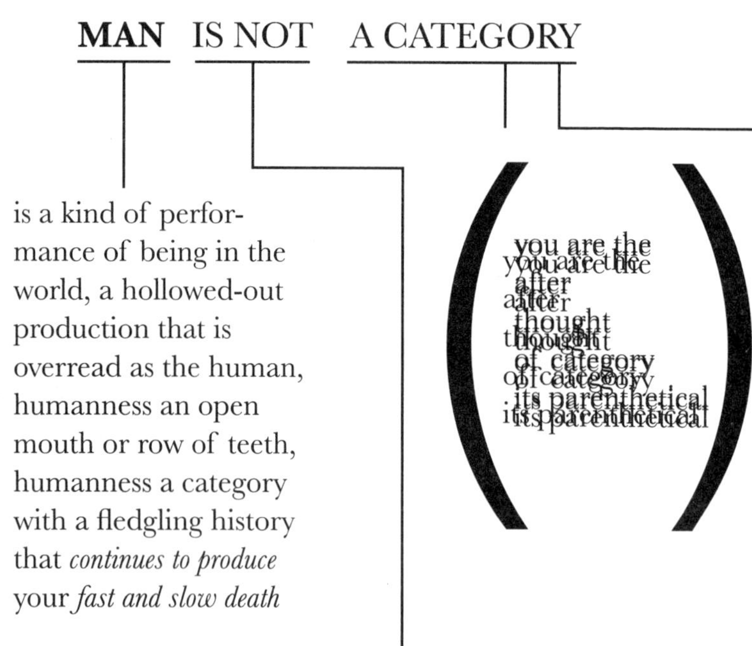

our effacement something incommensurable with description; your child once asked you *how old will you have been today*—the order in their time-based inquiry disrupted—you do not know the order, if Jerry is going or coming from the streetcar his body is not there, his ~~body~~ is removed

THAT INTERESTS YOU—

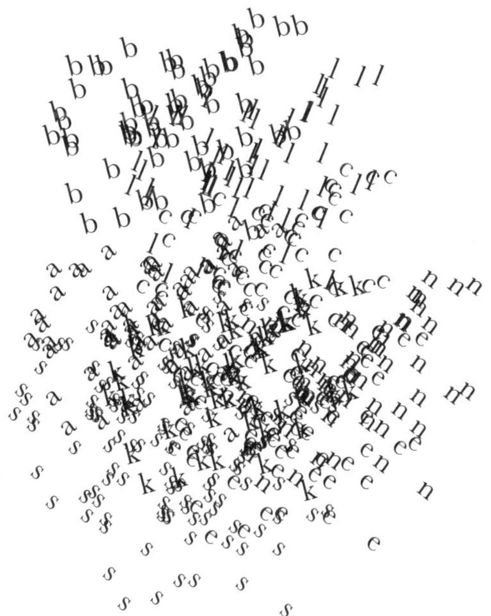

DIES

no one makes it out of here alive,
and then there are those who did
not make it here living, whose
deaths occur postmortem

DIES

you want to invert the word, either to signal its reversal or to make death a contronym, that those who have been refrained from life may also be its chorus

—**AFTER** **ILLNESS**, YOU PRESUME A TIME

of short duration, in
his body, *is* his body;
when man dies after
illness of short dura-
tion, it is really the
man who is of short
duration

of birth for Jerry
all you are able
to find is the record
of his death
the census data
stuttering over years:
1891 or 1889; there is far
more precision over his
death, accounting
for the removal
of his body
from a time
when it was
supposedly here

WHEN YOU ARE NOT ILL, YOU ARE NOT

stuck at the cause of his sudden death not being
determined, you are unsure what would
be determined that would satisfy you,
you are stuck, held hostage
by a grammar that refuses
to determine what
is killing
you

you say death
what you really
mean is time

OF THE HERE NOW FUTURE

you are not searching for redemption or the affirmation of having referent; you see yourself as though on your way to work, already half a ghost, and as you linger here it is not to recover what is already gone, you linger here to sketch the shape of undetermined death because gone might be the only available arrival

YOU ARE OF THE GONE

SHORT AS IN THE REMAINS OR WHAT

what remains / on the train / on the tracks / what haunts / is just underneath the skin / remembered within the cells / what spells are in your name / what is the *changing same* / what intrudes / spills from the body / from the grammar / from time / what persists / lingers / is just on the tip of your tongue / what debris / what rubble / what fragment / torn / and timeworn / what loss echoing until it reaches you

IS LEFT FROM WHAT IS CUT

becoming
s wav
whe
me t d had man

of his sudden death

an

rk, resident
s, died

street car
he Union
mployed

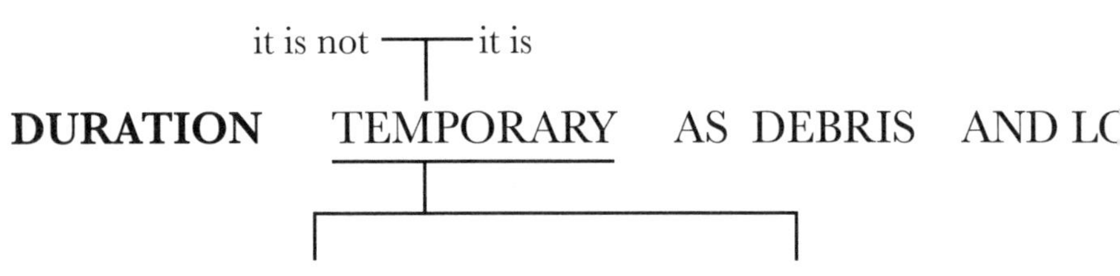

to extract,
names from
worn papers
that can't give
cause,
their suddenness,
is only a
narrow passage to
names,

to learn
your kin who
are unable to represent
a full account,
leaving you with
this loss
glimpsing through (a)
dark screen(s) where
the names, just fade

no matter how minor the debris,

AS THE CONDITIONS THAT MAKE IT

is evidence of something that remains, it is not just remains, it remains and here you are, a nodal point among the remains of the fraught sentences that led you here (led to you), their duration like the relative pitch between one body and another, Jerry a note with too long an interval between you; you are note and interval, you are relative and remains, how to end this sentence, or stretch it until it buckles beneath the weight of pronoun and participle and predicate, breaking, and there in the break is where you enter the underground where the slant rhyme of your body is not *illness* or *man* is not *after* or *death* is not *short* or *duration*, it is all of these things and their syntactical limit

PHOTOGRAPH
REGINALD JERRY CLARK
YEAR UNKNOWN
SAINT PAUL, MN

DREAM SEQUENCE #2

this is to indicate an/other territory. an inside seeing, a world making where someone is walking—between both here & there, somnambulant. something fading by degree. we look, we look but where the looking is directed is where the retina meets the optic nerve. we see but the seeing is an antebiological accumulation. within the aperture, retreating before our eyes someone is sleep-deprived, someone is sleeping amid the terror, someone is asleep & making a world.

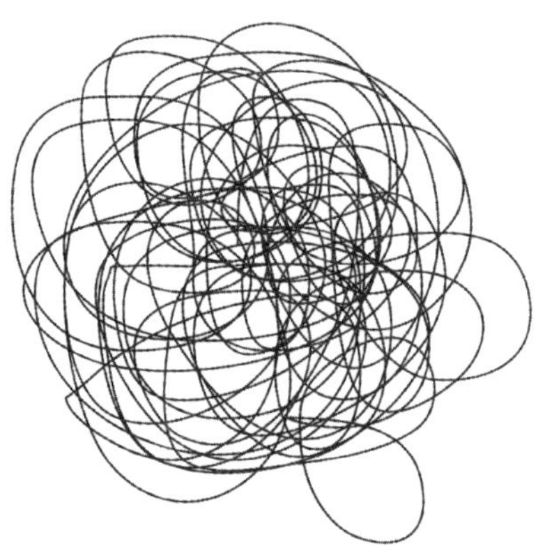

You have to look where it ain't.

—The Kentifrica Project

in the beginning . . . there was blackness to borrow some Ellisonian sermonics, done here to think with its *Now black is . . . an' black ain't* some slim attempt at articulation about the limits of articulation, which is here gesturing toward the border of a grammar and about the capacity of the photograph to retrieve what is in excess of the sign. i suppose there should be an admission that just as the photo is conditioned by what is outside of it, i am outside these margins setting the conditions for what comes in and out of view. this *i* will appear here only, an appeal to your trust, even as you are here being told the speaker means to lie to you . . .

we privilege the ocular, as though the eye were incapable of doing anything but telling the truth. as though we could not really know a thing outside the precincts of what we see. the photo then, following this logic and as modern document, is the preeminent *trustworthy* narrator. it holds a World, the World of the photograph being a containing force structuring a kind of field of possibility. you keep returning to the photo and to what it tells you, its shorthands and substitutions. you keep traveling from the nodal point of the photographic image, wondering if there might be more appropriate terms than the *real* both inside and outside of its zone of containment.

the grammar of the image, this slippery desire that reaches for what it cannot hold, what it cannot properly name, is what you spend many nights attempting to reconcile, is what you eventually come to regard as irreconcilable. you try to hold your gaze on what will supposedly register experience. you remain without lexical referent.

the image in question—some presupposed whole—is of your grandfather, whom you only know through the photo, a mythic knowledge of geneaology structured by the limits of the vocabulary your mother frames the image with, another *in the beginning was* laying down a set of tracks leading from the photographic image back (or is it forward?) to you.

Look!

Reginald's back is resting against the sofa. he is wearing a collared shirt and suspenders. in his hands there is a newspaper. you can only make out partials of two words: *bio* and *LAB*. the photo offers no indication of time, which is to say, you are unsure whether this marks the beginning of his work day or its end. he is wearing glasses, perhaps for the purpose of reading, but it is his eyes that give you pause, it is his eyes where your own looking begins. they are partially open (or is that closed?), the exhaustion that they say is without saying, is beyond saying. the eyes are not open and they are not closed, they are an interstice, a position that fixes his body to that room, and forms an escape route from it.

in *Magical Habits*, Monica Huerta writes *a photograph is like a poem: it betrays its limit by announcing that it is the limit.* here you agree with Huerta, that the photo entices a relationship to the real, to what has happened by its enclosure, as the poetic constraint seduces a reading by virtue of its form. this limit and its enunciation need the open eye. what does Reginald fail to see with his eyes partially closed? what is only seen by way of their near closure?

you are unsure how to resist the seduction of the image. your maternal grandfather is gone. there are instances in which you are uncertain of what it means to be here, how we understand ourselves to be substantiated within World, with the world of the photograph. is it corporeal, or is a body not enough to make definite one's hereness? you hear Pusha T in the background saying, *i can disappear, i swear*. something strained in the articulation, string stretching until one object is two, a pulsing in the lower registers pulling against and merging with a knowledge that where the grammar of World is involved, its possibility is found in your negation.

your mother tells you of photographs taken or lost by robbery or a succession of moves (she cannot say for sure). you know of them but do not have them. what is gone is always spectral, is always an impetus for the speculative. you draw a series of boxes that you understand to be missing photos, attempt to describe what is not there.

see a train coiling itself around a field, its many cars a body, its composition lacking a clear indication of a head or tail. no, see a tongue painting acrylic on some all-black surface, circle on concentric circle. no, no, see something dead lying on the tracks, its slowly withering corpse a part of the necro biome, an unliving mass lying in wait for the tight-grasping talons of some predator. or see none of these, or see all of these like a palimpsest or a sentence resisting punctuation.

he is standing. whole body blurred in double exposure. you cannot situate this image. it is unstable, a discongruous form that you understand as such by discrete borders. and so you speculate that moving into this fog is like traveling down a road where the end of your field of vision is swallowed by a thick brush. you try to unswallow the end of what you cannot see. spit it out, the whole taxonomy.

Look!

it is the debtors train. spectral rail. sleeping car. moving ontology. revisited abduction. requisite absence. choreography of death. mortuary grammar. it is swallowed years. it is always disappearance. the here gone and the gone gone. it is breath ended postmortem. it is to not be here, it is to be here in ways you cannot tell. it is to know the telling as a haunting also. it is arrested movement. missing time. the end of the line. it is every robbery. it is why you think about World's end. it is a collection of absences, somewhere between arrival and without terminus.

there is no correct, which is to say, precise and singular, way of naming what (who?) is in the photograph. this is a problem of representation, perhaps of memory and meaning. you do not know Reginald outside a series of fragments, stories and images. none of these alone or collectively materializes a body, gone already. you know this is an impossibility, yet it does not stop you from desiring to move through a sepia photo and touch his weary flesh. you imagine yourself entering the holes of this language as falling into the gaps in memory, as entering the cavity of awakeness and dreaming captured in Reginald's nearly closed eyes. it is there you see not a body, but form's precondition and limit. it is there you realize optics are contorting everything.

why do we keep coming back here?

Look!

you cannot properly represent what lacks a literal referent. Warren teaches you this, that the black figure is without place. but this is not just a black figure, it is your grandfather. and part of you recognizes you have been searching for meaning within the borders of the photograph. something that will make sense of the scale of what has been lost. a trail of evidence that will solve the heartache. and though you recognize that what you are looking for is without place and referent, and therefore without meaning, you are still grasping for something, some mutual embrace, poor pessimist that you are, knowing that nothing is there, the there-ness in this case being the contradiction.

what happens when we begin to disorder the whole? what can be known in the space of the hole hold?

strain & pulse &
full & merge &
pull & strain &
pulse & strain &
merge & full &
strain & pull &
pulse & full & full
& full & merge pull strain pulse

Fanon believed the dreams of the colonized to be muscular. you dream a territory, or perhaps beyond one. a phantom geography full of spectral things with which you are entangled. you are dreaming. you are unaware of where this places you on some timeline, if there is one. when and where do dreams happen? you have no address for this but you witness—an imaginative act—some chain reaction causing a train to explode. you take a seat to watch it bloom. when you awaken, you are a burned archive.

unspool
the dream
as though
its wreck
were
record

if someone is restricted from sleeping is told that any reprieve during long hours overnight across miles will be punished will be cut from too-thin wages if their body is pushed to exhaustion to the point that remaining photographic records of them often show eyelids just nearly closed if someone is so tired has not slept in so long they wear bone-weary as a garment are confused as to whether they are sleeping or awake have looped interruptions of time are arriving unaware of how they got here are not here at all are a wraith or some unaccounted freight if someone's sleep is stolen hours garnished over decades until their body is some kind of corporeal debt is completely withdrawn is gone does their exhaustion have a name?

perhaps its proper name is ghostly.

the black historical is already the hauntological.

and through the slippage—a specter of what is nearly open or nearly closed—we enter, as though climbing into an underground cavern. we do not know—the eyes have been lying, have been our primary source of knowing, but we are moving aboard the complex ruins of a train, or is it a body? we are moving toward the edge of something, outside its edges, beyond a boundary. at first we came to attempt to raise the dead and could not. had we been able to we could have asked him things, removed his glasses, covered him with a blanket. we presupposed something about what constitutes life. about who is alive. we were moving toward its edges, failing to pull anything through the veil. and now we are moving toward the edge of something to fail, to critically examine our own fidelity to those edges, to failure. for a moment we are nearly opening and nearly closing our eyes; not real, not becoming, perhaps not even here, always already ghostly. and within that near closure, that near opening we gather some trace evidence of our gone and we Look! where it ain't, we Look! even if it isn't.

PHOTOGRAPH
REGINALD JERRY CLARK
YEAR UNKNOWN
SAINT PAUL, MN

DREAM SEQUENCE #3

a rope-like finger of wind & sky. which is perhaps an attempt at absurdity, it is to envisage the embodiment of the storm. it is by slow decay or sleight of hand or other cunning to reorder an image placed in sequence, to undiscipline the visual from its articulations until Reginald Jerry Clark is not the weary laborer, the black rail worker, whose restless graveyard shifts are themselves the slow accruement of a tomb. no, in a year unknown we are seeing a slender digit crack through the ceiling of the world, intent on touching something.

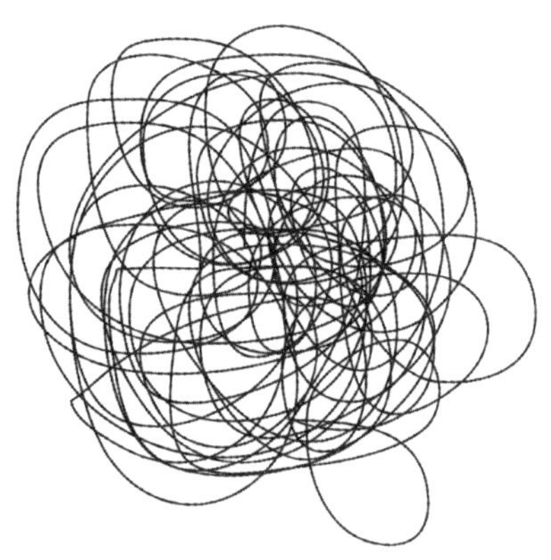

I think I am possessed by my mother's dispossession, and her mother's, and her mother's . . .

—Moon Charania

. . . that's all them bastards have left us: words.

—Derek Walcott

non sense

is

when you are young your mother tells you stories in order to correct you, or provide instruction. these stories hold a loose relationship with what has happened, their multiplicity are many tongues in her mouth. when you are older you think of their kaleidoscope telling as lies, not because they are untrue but because they are a train moving in two directions at once. one story was of your great-uncle or grandfather, depending on the telling, and how his thumb was bit off by a squirrel, the lesson being, to stay away from squirrels, the lesson being, your mother believed there to be a variety of species, seemingly harmless, that would prowl after your body, would consume it one digit at a time. when you are older, you tell your children about the squirrel and laugh, you still shudder considering the prowling.

squirrels chirp and chatter, the trill of their tongues both music and alarm. their *wrruhhing*, moaning voices a chorus of rumors, maybe about the tree canopy or the food stowed away. some have been known to scream.

you grew up pentecostal, sharing sundays with black factory workers and truck drivers, black teachers and kitchen workers who had labored tirelessly throughout the week, whose bodies knew sweat and exaustion yet were not empty. they would untrain their torsos from regimen, tilting them, slanting their backs and lifting their heads in ecstatic rapture. you would join the congregation and untrain language from its procedures, speaking in other tongues, ones you did not know, your trembling lips a doorway for the holy ghost. in so many ways it seemed that the flailing bodies and the disordered sound that emerged from them, the wail and wonder that were coterminus in that raucous sunday worship were an aesthetic practice that suspended the exhuastion of the week, its logic and order, and drew from disarticulation.

your mother taught you to speak in tongues, a practice relying less on your knowing than on your letting go of your knowing. not a mother tongue. not a tongue of origin. she taught you to story, to move through the crossroads of speech, Esu Elegbara, forked articulation. your mother taught you to speak in tongues, and at present you cannot speak with her. this not speaking a chasm neither of you knows how to cross. what is loss but a chasm. a rift between places or bodies? or perhaps it is more accurate that the rift is not between the bodies, but in them. in this way loss is a hunger and the hole is not out there. it is a deep cavern inside you. you are ravenous.

she names you chaun, pronounced *shaun*, says that god told her to spell your name this way, that it was preordained. these odd spellings, spells, is just the way your mother speaks, taking one word and making it another. the hard consonants that she tells you are the material god gives her for your name are something stumbled over in every first class, on most documents. the TSA agent looks at you, and then your ID, calls you *chaaoon*. you don't correct them, your name a secret language between you and your mother. we make of ourselves old testament gods magnificent and vengeful, naming is our power and with it we animate the vast nothing. bible is Babel is babble. you make and you are made. you author characters, new Ezekiels surrounded by dry bones, you give them half lives, and then, destruction. you unmake as well. it is not long before you are a nonbeliever, before you dethrone this god in your mouth. but you still babble, tongue quaking, you jump into the dark pool of what you cannot language. *shatasolodana*. you unsay, or you sound a thing. you try to make a hard consonant soft. you stumble.

you cannot speak with your mother, you do not know how to make something soft of this hard consonant. it is an absence blaring in every room, a riot in some unseen throat. you imagine your ghosts this way, not like the specters in movies where their arrival is marked by soft music or the creaking of floorboards or an expansive silence. your ghosts are screaming, and their silence is also loud.

your youngest child has a habit of confusing subject with object pronouns, common in child language acquisition. *baba*, they ask you, *is her there*? as you both observe an old photograph of your mother. *no baby, she was there, in the army.* you think the photo was taken in germany. and you pause a moment to think those three words they use to form their question: *is her there*, no subject in the sentence, just the her of the photographic image suspended between being and location, is-ness and there-ness, how there are allowances for these disorderings as children, a certain innocence in the confusion. but as an adult to disorder subject and object or to rearrange the sentence, *her is there, there her is, her there, her is*, is to disrupt a linguistic commitment to coherence, to completion, and to reason. her isn't there, her isn't anywhere relationally locatable for your child, in ways Reginald was not for you. the coordinates you have gathered are through silences and their seldom interruptions. *baby, her is not there, but we can try to find her.*

s her there there her is her there there her is there her is there there her is there there her there her is there there her is her is there there her there h

her there there her is her there there her is there there her is there her is there there her is her is there there her there her is her your mother talks in rumors. of other genealogical lines. of how you were born in the veil. you can *see* things she says. you can *know* things. a stress in the articulation of S-E-E things and K-N-O-W things. like there is something unaccounted for that you might name, that you might behold.

you want to see where the train first derails, you want to know where the limb is first removed, but this is the wrong question.

is her

is

is her
is there her there
is her
there
there
is
her is
her is
is there
is
her
there
is
her
her is

her is her is her is her is her is her is

her is

her there

there her
there
there
her is her there there her is her there her is
is
is her
there
her
is
is her

there

it is the story of the thumb, of its removal from the hand, of some diminished dexterity—*who was it again?* she tells you *your great-uncle*—that *a squirrel bites it off*—a story of removal of a diminished hand—*but a squirrel, how does it do this?* you do not perceive the same danger. you are told of how a squirrel will dig its teeth into and through the bone—*but who? your grandfather*—*thumb bitten*—*some hand*—she tells you—how diminished dexterity—removal of some great-uncle—again the story—*how does it do this?* you are told *danger*—*biting the hand*—*your grandfather*—*but who?* remove the story—told *dig*—*will hand*—*will teeth*—*will tell it.*

tell it.

one of the fundamental principles that you learned growing up was that your mother's power as a parent came from her assertion that she could unmake you. *i brought you into this world, and i can take you out.* it is haunting as an adult to think of your child self being told that an error of childhood, or maybe *the* error of childhood, would incite so much anger in the person who birthed you that they would wish you unmade, more so that they would wish themselves the instrument of your unmaking. dramatic speech, yes. hyperbole, often. but also violence. a violence that was accompanied by stick or cord or belt to flesh anytime you were off track. you were often off track.

i love my mother i fear my mother i love my mother i fear my mother i love my mother i am afraid.

if grammar is the structure housing your speech, making the labor of it possible, then you wonder if blackness is the grammar of loss in the modern world, the primary signifier for loss's dispossessing torque, blackness structuring the relationship between owning and owned. *you had a grandfather.* a sentence aiming at a kind of ownership, but the pastness of the verb is a geography too distant, sand sifted between your fingers no matter how tightly you clench them. *had* marks death. you have a mother, and yet here in this present you cannot possess, own, or even hold her. you have a mother, and she is gone. you wonder if it would feel easier if you had made it so, that if by changing mother into modder into other into moth, the damage would feel less heavy, the record less threadbare. perhaps we have all been had, gotten over, by the archive and the slippery words that make blackness known only when it is *about to disappear*. as a writer you feel responsible to make something happen, to have something appear before the reader. here is Reginald, or there he was. does this place you in the tradition of hunting fugitive slaves, of policing the black body's appearance? can a black body not be opaque? your dance instructor tells you that dance is all material, that in its body forwardness it is only realized at the moment of its disappearance. you and your kin are the pre- and postperformance of absence, this dance a knapsack of language you are left with. you do not consent to these words, and these words are all you have.

LANGU NGUISH

one of the fundamental principles that you learned growing up was not to speak ill of family. especially not in mixed company. you are breaking the contract here. once, your mother broke the contract also: it is a moment you won't fully recount. she would name an experience with her father—your grandfather whom you've spent the last decade writing and thinking on—where he almost took her life. this would break with other kinds of stories where you could only faintly trace the shape of the past. it was a moment where the past would spill out of your mother unaware, as the too heaviness of history often does. she would tell you of this life-threatening encounter with her father in a way where you could recognize his rage, its misdirection a runaway train, how your mother and her sisters would be collateral damage. she would not say this to you in a way where she would recognize the shadow of this fury in herself, how the train would keep moving through her.

i love my mother i fear my mother i love my mother i fear my mother i love my mother i am afraid.

—the cracked sound—the strained note—the unmemory you keep trying to name—the train—the strained—*no*—the stutter—the disordered sequence of what you utter—the tear in the page—the train—the strained sound—the name cracked—unmemory sequenced through a tear—a note—sounding in the page—strain the sequence—the cracked utterance—the train—the strain—the train—sequen—train—ing—dysfluen—name—crack—it—open—it's all sound

your grandfather worked as a porter for the Great Northern Railroad for twenty-five years. working for white folks who would call him boy and George and nigger and boy and anything but Reginald. denied rest in life, died seven months after retirement, and, as far as you can tell, before ever receiving his pension. you have been examining these details these past ten years, rearranging them, theorizing on them. what you have failed to examine is how the train cars of bitterness your grandfather was made to swallow, the swell of anger, was a bill your mother had to pay, that she should not have had to pay. and as an extension you have been left with some of the balance. you are unsure of how to get off these tracks, to not be some additional train car, to stop building the railroad. your grandfather was robbed of time and dignity and pension, the train he was aboard undid him, but it was not the train that almost killed your mother, it was your grandfather. and as you learn to grieve for your mother as an unprotected child, you are also reckoning with how it was not your grandfather who laid hands on you.

i love my mother i fear my mother i love my mother i .
love my mother i am afraid.

the shortcomings of language have you returning to tongues, due to how ill-equipped you feel langauge is to recount or explain so many things. tongues is excess, and when you superimpose the text in the poem or sentence so that one word is bleeding, colliding into another and another until they are not distinct units any longer but a singular plural, you understand yourself to be speaking in tongues. these textual tongues disorient the axis of the graphic unit, when you stretch the text beyond the parameters of the margins, exceeding them, it is much like how you conceive of blackness: as beyond knowing, as outside the parameters of intelligible grammar. this is not a mother tongue, it is an irreverent one that you are attempting to proceed with, unsure where it will lead, unsure of what it is even saying. your mother gifted you this also, this glossolalic trembling of tongues. you love her, and fear her, which is your most essential loneliness. you wonder if a train can cross this incommensurable fissure. what if these tongues and their strain are train cars riding midair across the breach, you don't know where they go or if they will reach her. if you were to name your desire, foolish as you think it is, you imagine them traveling backward and forward at once, to you and your mother and her father and all our many kin for whom you have faint or no record at all. you cast your tongues to name what cannot be named, to move into the abstraction one train car at a time, beyond articulation, and yet here your trembling tongues keep saying, keep disarticulating something you want to hold, that you want to be held by; you are casting tongues in a space you cannot see beyond to experiment with exhaustion, you are so very exhausted, but what you mean is that you want to bring this language and all it thinks it knows off the tracks of that knowing until all that is left is what we've hidden, not *from* but *for* each other.

strain the history through the holes in your trembling tongues,
refuse the terms of its order, make the story stutter.

stutter.

tell it again.

in another telling of the story she says it was a rabbit that bit off Reginald's thumb—*mama do you remember talking of a great-uncle?—it was your grandfather—what bit?—a rabbit*—and here you imagine the trickster star-hero brer lying in wait in a thicket, biding their time in the brush in a space less known and unmapped, and perhaps here as in a folktale, the rabbit is a figure—*do you really remember this? are you making this up? are we not always?*—the encounter with the rabbit like the stories she tells makes you feel less sure of who is speaking—of who is feeding and who is feast. Syke would take the surname Fox—another figure—and perhaps these many tellings—the split tongue of them—the ecology of rumor that they compose—are the only inheritance you might pick up like so many missing limbs.

fugitive

pre
sence.

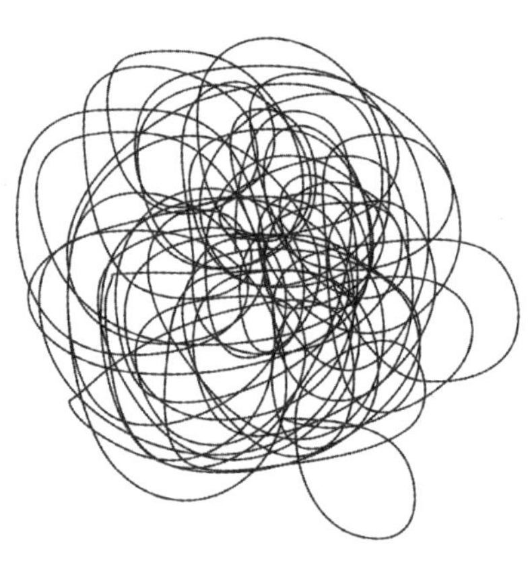

Alice

dear Alice, i saw you the other day sitting on a swing.
you have many letters beginning with a variation of this.

dear Alice, how high has the chariot taken you?
dear Alice, when you are lifting, are you looking or do you close your eyes?

dear Alice, i miss you.

you did not know your great grandmother Alice, daughter of Augustus and Addie, granddaughter of the first Fox, Syke. but you know her. you know the scent of cinnamon from her salt-pepper hair, tied in a bun. you know the melody of how she would call your mother's name, how something would descend and rise in her tone. you know there is a way to look that exceeds seeing what is in the visual field. she saw everything. you imagine she sees you—you are seeing her also—her eyes two planets you are orbiting, and when you look, Alice is in you and you in Alice, a tightly woven network of pronouns, the link chains of a swing.

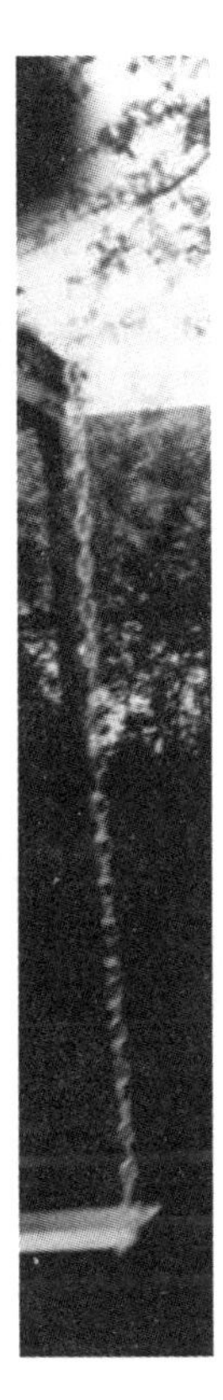

SWING LOW

there is something about Moses Sumney's voice as you are listening to "Bystanders (in space)." something arresting in its pitch, the channel it crosses between the overdetermined sign of vocal masculinity and femininity. hybrid. the high falsetto of *oh you wanna strip away* and you do, you want to eliminate every artifice you raise between the song and your flesh, between the sound and the current of feeling its dense geography erects.

what can be hidden underneath a note? what can swing below its surface with a knapsack of secrets in tow?

Moses descends with

don't waste your candor on bystanders

it will be the lowest vocal register of the song and its duration transforms the distance these six words may traverse. by the time we have been brought before the bystanders, Moses has taken us lower than would feel consistent with standing. we are

knocked and

kneeling and

lower.

and in this low space of Moses's voice, at times holding verbal expression in inarticulation, in the black bottom of its telling, nonspeech is its swing, a dissatisfaction with a single position of meaning, undulating, a train moving in two directions.

and here *low* does not get to the bottom of it, a swing that in its descent brings your feet close to a kind of ground that they cannot touch, and as it swings never reaching the surface, there is only the strained sense that the bleeding edges of sound can untrain a strict commitment to the vocabulary that gives it shape.

SWEET CHARIOT

a train is not a chariot. Jerry would take a K line from Louisiana, Missouri, to Keokuk, Iowa, to see you, a course enslaved black folks in Missouri had also taken in flight from captivity, composing escape routes with their bodies. a train is not a chariot, unless it is underground, unless it has swung low. Jerry worked the K line, made the trip, tucked a little money away, made a return trip and back again. Alice, you were his terminus. you would marry, a few would witness you would witness each other, two sentences entangled like your braided hair.

a braid wraps around, goes over and under, between and through. a braid resists the categorical distinction of a strand's singular line.

take your chariot. dig your heels into the soil. lean back until your body has flown before the foundational hydrogen and helium and lithium. be your own black beginning of the universe. now swing low and sweep on past ages to a polyrhythm syncopating between you and your lover exiting the train.

but Alice, i saw you the other day sitting on a swing, and the swing beside you was empty, and your eyes carried the freight of accumulated years.

COMING FOR

the momentum of the song sways on the axis of the words *bystanders* and *waste*

don't waste your candor on bystanders

and as the chariot of the song climbs higher

they'll watch you wasteawaywasteawaywasteaway

waste as in trash, what we designate to be discarded, or perhaps there is a way to think waste as excess, as that which lies outside of easy quantification or brings it before its mathematical limit.

and this they, bystanders on whom candor should not be wasted, for they'll watch you wasting—a kind of preperformance—before deciding to use one's own body for inertia to catch the wind, to take flight.

TO CARRY

dear Alice, i feel like a bystander, someone who is off to the side, watching. unable to intervene.

but this is likely placing too hard a boundary between death and aliveness, between a past and what might constitute this present.

dear Alice, i saw you the other day, but no matter how hard i tried to animate the image or climb into the photograph, to fill the swing beside you with my body, it remains empty. dear Alice, do not waste away.

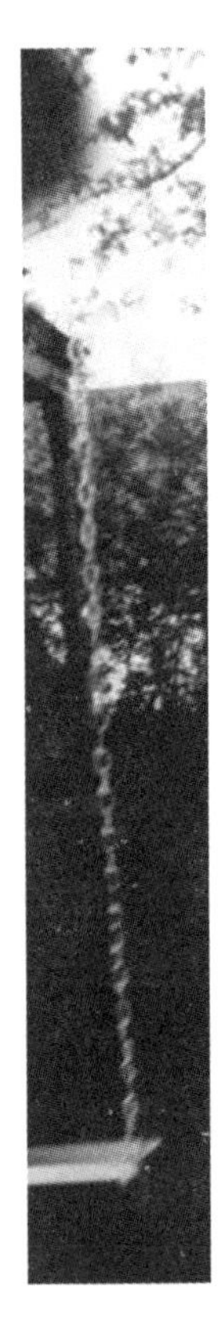

ME HOME

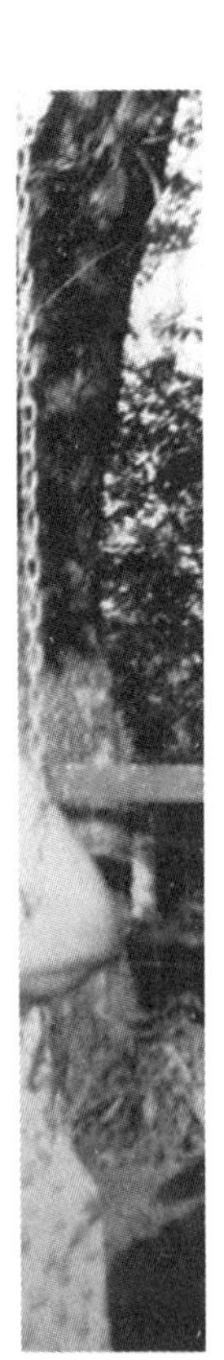

you outlived your husband, Jerry, and your elder son, Reginald, both taken by the train, both trained to shrink and not to swing. the other day i saw you sitting on a swing, Alice, but when i close my eyes boarding the chariot of some hybrid vocal register, its highs and lows, i am there with you, the blur of our bodies moving not across but between time.

swing low sweet chariot,
there are no bystanders here.

PHOTOGRAPH
REGINALD JERRY CLARK
YEAR UNKNOWN
SAINT PAUL, MN

DREAM SEQUENCE #4

there is a child standing in a field. a universe unto themselves, or rather a part—entangled—both in & of the field. terrible. beautiful. this child, standing, staring at the field—at themselves—a kind of territory, unmapped and not a country. this child moving away or toward—it becomes unclear in the temporal logics imposed. no it is not toward, no it is not away, it is both & neither. in fact after extended observation it is not a child nor a field. it is nothing at all, & everything too.

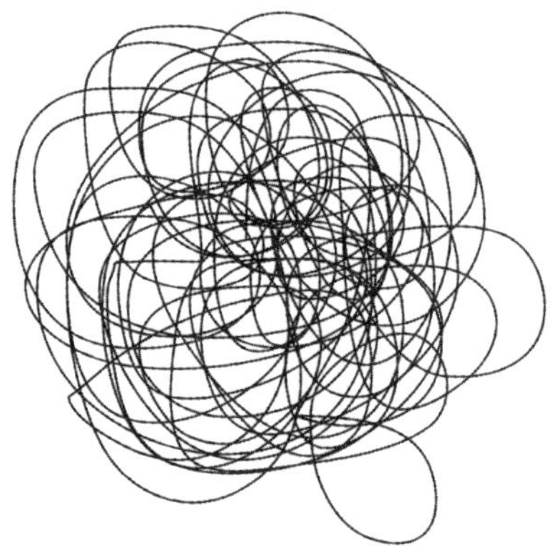

We do not ride on the railroad; it rides upon us.

—Henry David Thoreau

the first time that you remember riding a train, you were trying to perform a magic trick. you had a deck of cards and on the back of the cards were these nondescript symbols that help the magician identify each card's number and suit. for weeks you had been studying these symbols and by the time of the train ride you were able to read them from any position. when you have a willing participant you tell them that you can name any card that they pull from the deck. they have heard this before but you are young so they indulge you. how you pull them into the trick is through the common grammar that you build in your looking, or rather in how you look past.

---

it is a calculated disinterest that you display in what they have pulled; you are practiced in collecting peripheral information. this data can be collected as you discuss the weather, the mystery of a cloud's shape so often mimicking what we call it by, or the mass of metal moving us from one geography to another. you bring them close, close enough to mimic a kind of intimacy. it is an agreement that we are making one with another: that the only lies told here will be honest ones.

---

the last time you remember riding a train you were with your child, riding the rail from the Minneapolis airport, attuning them to the stillness of your bodies, a sensation juxtaposed with the fast-moving machine carrying you. you tell them, *baby close your eyes and we'll try and feel the wind against our faces.* neither of you can see or feel the wind, but with your eyes closed you almost catch a glimpse of its shape as it moves across the territory of your body. it is only as the officer approaches, asking for evidence of your payment that you realize you have forgotten to swipe your metro card. they lecture you with their hand on their weapon about swiping each time, how your lapse was a kind of theft. they tell you they'll let you go with a warning.

---

what is the distinction between being a passenger and freight? the train transports both, but perhaps this is the wrong question. you see the protections afforded to freight, just as to the passenger, but as the officer approached, you felt the out-of-placeness of your body, the shift in your tone being dialed to deferential. you had paid for your metro card, you had only failed to swipe it, yet the officer felt the need to deliver you their lecture—hand on holster—on theft, on the proprietary nature of passage. you are not a passenger, and you are not freight, your body is situated in a nonplace aboard the train, and even this nonplace has been stolen.

---

pick a card, any card, and when they have the card committed to memory and place it back into the deck (not once have you lost their eyes) you are still gathering what you need to know, the information beneath the surface. you shuffle the cards and tell them a story about the time you snuck out the window of your room in the second story of your house with a blanket you thought could parachute you safely to the ground. you didn't jump, but sometimes you dream of yourself floating from that rooftop. you describe the feeling of weightlessness, say each word with a slow precision, make the words into a stairwell they climb to bring us closer to each other, weightless and parachuting back to the ground.

---

did you have the nine of clubs?

---

you have a child who is fascinated by trains—read backward—there is a great grandchild to your maternal grandfather who is fascinated by trains. after the track is laid and the train cars are placed on it your child will repetitively position something ahead of the cars' arrival: several blocks or a book or a body part. they love watching the collision. sometimes you hear them in the other room laughing at another derailing. you yourself have a fascination with reading about train wrecks, the way bearing failure or a dragging undercarriage might catapult a train car, but more arresting is the way something whole is pulled apart beyond recognition.

---

in 1968, a month after the assassination of Dr. King, another murder less reported on would happen. the writer Henry Dumas would move through a turnstile at a New York City subway station. while aboard the train a traffic cop would fatally shoot him in the chest. some reports say he had a knife or a pistol or that he was in an argument with a passenger. or Henry Dumas was simply black aboard a train and his body a train car left unsecured until collision. Toni Morrison would call him *genius, an absolute genius* and she would wish *he were around now to help us straighten out the mess*. but you wonder if this mess is a condition beyond straightening as you board, or rather are already aboard, the train as well.

you have watched more train shows with your child than you can count. *Thomas*, and *Dinosaur Train*, *Robot Train & Friends*, and *Mighty Express*. so much play and pleasure in the locomotive, so much enchantment. and in america this seems to be the formula, to entangle the violence with delight until we ourselves are laying the tracks of our undoing. once, you attempted to hide every toy train in your home. but you are complicit in purchasing them. you both keep finding yourselves in play. pain

---

sometimes you are the train as you move your child from one side of the house to the other, whistling, then saying, *all aboard!* they board you and you give them passage, back to the other side and again. sometimes the terminus is the mall, other times it is not a place but a direction, *up!* or *over there!* again and back. this is a repetition you are trying to disrupt. you want to give your child passage as something other than the train.

steel

stolen

still

Jerry left Missouri to work the train. his son, your grandfather, would work the train, black stolen aboard black steel / moving moving black steel / the stolen abducted into alteration review the molecules moving moving steel / no sleep wake stolen slow shattering of physiology steel / slow slow moving stolen razed bodies of the raised and fallen sun steel / the clenched heart constricted beating the disruption and decimation of the nonsensate steel / moving moving steel / stolen light steel / the cells of the unmoving bodies ruined and undone steel / the end and the beginning too steel / loss until its event-based logics are incommensurate with the black stolen moving moving steel / and stolen and still.

---

fuck a train.

---

i'll walk to where i'm heading next.

---

you say, *the people get tired of dying*. we so tired of watching ourselves be undone, our unliving lives amounting to no more than a quarter mile of track. board the train, Henry, hold that pistol close as a prayer to usher in our rest. lay us to sleep. terminus. something of an end. an opening. a second act. we are tired of watching you, watching us board the train, a passage unspooling beyond grounds for return. dead reckoning. you never returned. we never arrived. we are watching the tired outline of our dying. & somewhere at the end of the line, we open our mouth, no longer a mouth but a steam trumpet, whistling, our buzzing lips assembling vibrations, a mass of impossible sound.

---

amen.

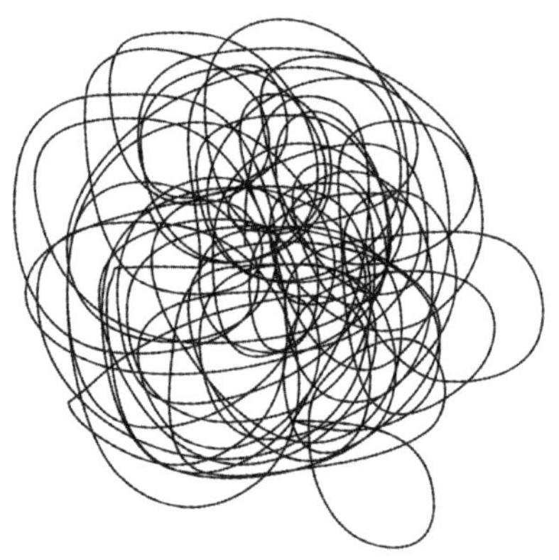

wherein a child writes a letter to undream themself from their grandfather:

Dear Reginald,

i have been trying to make you appear, a naive wish against this inherited melancholy, have been looking over the fragments of documents that are not you—a wallet, a time sheet, a notice of death—and thinking that through these remnants and the half stories they tell i might piece you back together. but you are not a wallet or a time sheet or a notice of death, and the severed record i have been left with is a poor mirror. Hartman was right, the facts are volatile, and the metaphors, impossible. at times i have felt the cracking of my voice as though yours or Alice's, Syke's or Hannah's has unknowingly spilt through its crevices, but you are not a ghost i want to continue to yield my tongue to. Reginald, i am sending you this letter, a missive, from the end rhyme of a wasteland, to undream myself from your record, unspool myself from this train of thought. the duration of the sentence, which is to say the battery acid of it that i've swallowed, has been too long.

c

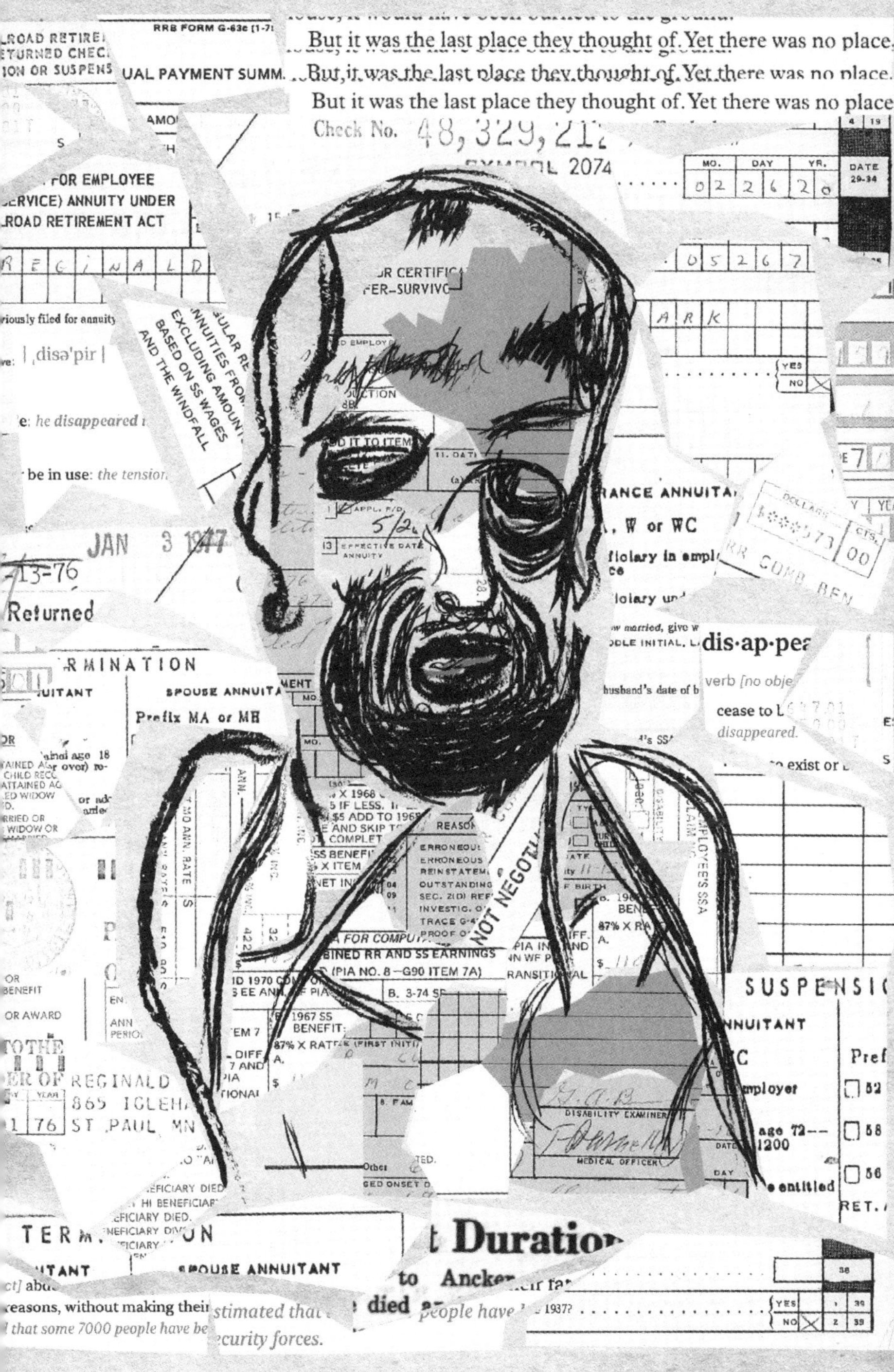
But it was the last place they thought of. Yet there was no place.
But it was the last place they thought of. Yet there was no place.
But it was the last place they thought of. Yet there was no place.
RRB FORM G-63c
UAL PAYMENT SUMM.
Check No. 48,329,21
SYMBOL 2074
MO. DAY YR.
DATE
FOR EMPLOYEE
SERVICE) ANNUITY UNDER
ROAD RETIREMENT ACT
REGINALD
viously filed for annuity
|disəˈpir|
he disappeared
be in use: the tension
JAN 3 1977
Returned
RMINATION
SPOUSE ANNUITANT
Prefix MA or MH
ULAR RE
ANNUITIES FROM
EXCLUDING AMOUNT
BASED ON SS WAGES
AND THE WINDFALL
RANCE ANNUITA
A, W or WC
husband's date of b
dis·ap·pea
verb [no obje
cease to b
disappeared.
to exist or
NOT NEGOTI
ERRONEOUS
REINSTATEMENT
OUTSTANDING
INVESTIG.
BINED RR AND SS EARNINGS
(PIA NO. 8 — G90 ITEM 7A)
1967 SS BENEFIT:
87% X RATE
TRANSITIONAL
DISABILITY EXAMINER
MEDICAL OFFICER
SUSPENSI
ANNUITANT
Employer
age 72
REGINALD
865 IGLEHA
ST. PAUL, MN
TERM ION
SPOUSE ANNUITANT
t Duration
to Ancker
died
reasons, without making their
that some 7000 people have be
stimated that
people have
curity forces.
YES
NO

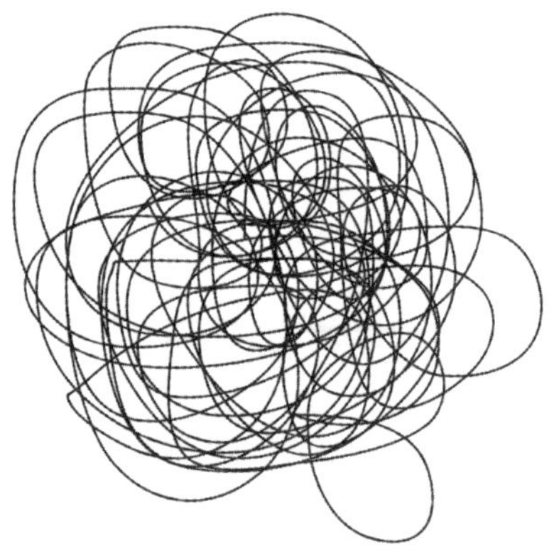

Hannah

h

is for *h*ow we draw a path
to each other, *h*ow that path
exceeds the line. it is for
*h*and and *h*eld and
*h*enceforth

n

is *n*ot seen *n*or sought from
the frayed accounts that
supposedly give us shape

a

*a*ll we *a*re *a*nd *a*ll we *a*in't
*a*nd everything in between

a

no *a*nswers to the questions
that *a*re being posed here
have been *a*rchived

h

*h*annah, if these words—
split and searching as they
are—should find you, meet
me somewhere outside the
ledger, a *h*aunting.

n

o archive would have ever
een sufficient

PHOTOGRAPH
REGINALD JERRY CLARK
YEAR UNKNOWN
SAINT PAUL, MN

DREAM SEQUENCE #5

& the child no longer standing, but running toward the storm. & by now what is seen & what is told are imbricated, are lying, are facing each other in a funhouse of mirrors waiting to see which vanishes first. Reginald, seizing the rare occasion of an escape route from the waking world—a fugitive act: to disappear & not be gone. a child, once standing in a field where our initial instruments of perception do not notice movement, cannot identify the squall doubling as cry & current, until something, still without grammar, shifts our technology of seeing, bringing the entire haunted world before our eyes, running toward the wind, becoming the storm.

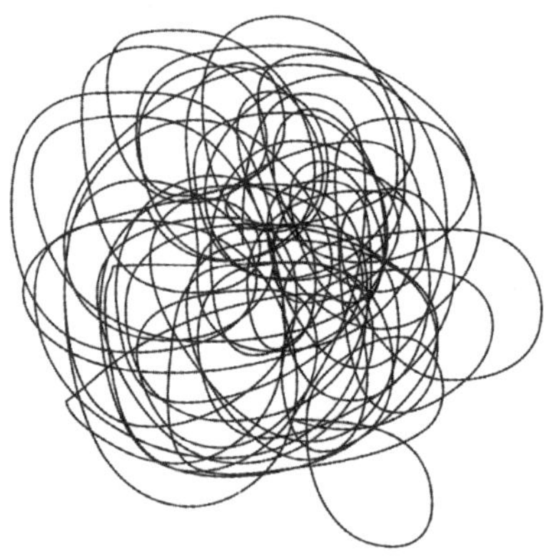

we are all haunted by blackness that never left,
what has never found rest . . .

—fahima ife

the black historical is already the hauntological: to be black in the world is to be a haunting. you heard something at a point of entry (not a beginning), a long hallway where sound echoes off an unknown object. they say an echo can be used to calculate the object's distance. how far gone are your gone? can you triangulate this ghostly matter? how would you know when you've found it? to be gone before you were here feels akin to abduction (alien), that first principle of blackness, perhaps of black presence: it's there and it ain't. to abduct, snatch, seize, hold hostage, kidnap, capture, to carry off. abduction is an imposing force or a beguilement, as when someone is told there will be a fair exchange for their labor, as when the snarl of hunger is the alternative to an uneven exchange. your maternal grandfather must have known this, must have understood something of the ransom of his body (but it is too early to be talking of bodies, or maybe it is too late). does a haunting require comprehension? you are not driven by what you know. it's the not knowing that's pulling you, that's moving this: you are compelled by the holes in your memory, your memory being against narrative composition, discontinuous threads you've attempted to braid and tear apart again. what do you remember? what don't you remember? can you name the not remembering? is there a grammar for it? you build a list, composing a possible vernacular for nothing: fraught, freight, fury, fail. you do not write *future*; futurity is for believers and you are not one. you are not. this goes back to the going, to the gone. you are partial to your absented kin. an absence—quiet as it's kept—though it be a hole in space, is not weightless. it is a hole and a whole sky. you cannot see its end. it is the failure of closure. maybe this is why you have been writing against the i, its conclusiveness: you are wanting to do violence to the so-called security it proposes, so you dive into the debris, attempting to make it disappear. attempting to make the other you, the reader who has confused this former you for themself, unstable. you, dear reader, are not safe here either. this does not end well, it does not end. you are a trace evidence of your maternal grandfather—a kind of remains—you are of his exhaustion, a faded though repeated pattern. you find yourself in the dream, in the liminal space between being asleep and awake, a spectral-ness to it, and like the blurred pictures that were passed on to you, the image is not quite clear. in these dreams you feel like a photograph of a photograph. even this body is a strange mythology, an early draft of a ghost. initially, you entered this hallway through genealogy, but now you are wandering through it, with no fixed address. listening to the muffled articulations of Reginald & Regina, Jerry & Alice, Syke & Hannah. these names blistering into collision, the crash of their sound cracking open until you cannot distinguish one from another. glossolalia. *eloshonobaba*, like when you would speak in tongues as a child, your black pentecostal breath an open mouth of cacophonous speech, your tongue a train car you permit the ghost to ride. do not say spirit, say ghost; more wail in ghost, more babble, more disorder from the protocols of language. the ghost is a fugitive, eluding capture. like the ghost, you know how to disappear. you've been watching slow disappearances all your life. your kin, inheritors of a centuries-long ghost protocol. some call it modernity. where do the disappeared go? are the gone, gone? or are they simply haunting on another register? you have written *nowhere* and *nothing* and *no one* so frequently, returned to the weight of these terms so often, that every syllable of them is in you. you make ruins of previous speech acts, ones you have cast down that long hallway wondering how they might return to you. the longer the sound takes to come back to you again, the less precise. but you have been practicing this imprecision, inasmuch as one can be a practitioner of the imprecise; you have been rehearsing something indistinct. you are not interested in accuracy. haunting does not forage from the factual, lies being in the bones of facticity too. you are in search of something unreliable, for the so-called reliability of the ledger, the archive, and the image is often a lie. you do not know all the dates, some paper trails have been eliminated, but even if they were complete, this would not be the measure of their truth. you are without the tools that you are told equip someone to make a claim. you are making claims. reading the photo negatives. retrieving the double exposure as a practice of pushing language beyond the limits of language. these outer limits of language are a spectral geography. the first time you remember encountering ghosts was as a child. your mother tells you you were no more than two years of age when you spoke to her of a moon with the face of a man who was threatening to kill you, or perhaps it just spoke to you of death, but your mother believed this detailed description to be beyond your fledgling imagination, or so the story goes. so there you were in your crib speaking with the moon about dying. your dreams would be the other frequent meeting place with your gone. a scene with your maternal grandmother, Dorthy, both of you in her volkswagen, you in the back seat picking at her moles as she sat in the front. you cannot see her face but you can feel her whole body smiling, you can smell smoke and sweet apples. she has long been gone. gone before the dream your mother tells you is a memory, before the dream-memory builds a temple for itself beneath your eyelids. you are laughing with her in this sanctuary of her volkswagen, the only church you both need, your laughter a kind of prayer. exceeding your language of description this dream temple is an abstract painting you carry within you, like those of Caroline Kent who paints toward a *representation of language free from lexical and syntactic limits*. the deep pool of her black canvas, an incubation for lexical and syntactic freedom. her shapes suggesting but not constituting written language are a dream geography and as such also a spectral one. this is the only way you can see yourself *moving through walls*, like Dana of *Kindred*, though you are not on a trip home, you are in a crib speaking with death—no, you are in a volkswagen with your nana—no, you are in the sleeping car of a train. without terminus. remember, this does not end well, it does not end. it is a sprawling list, a vernacular of silence, residual, interruption, attenuated, formless, record, constraint, inherit, medium, memory, evidence, deferred, hushed, repetition, interstice, immanent, uneven, allegory, speculative, line, intervening, letters, collecting, liminal, plural, atrocity, render, edge, grafting, absence, unreal, forgetting, past, assemblage, relation, belated, meaning. you unspool alongside this runaway vocabulary you are attempting to read, the residue it collects, a handful of time you are trying to suspend through sentence and line and paragraph. what might this inventory do? what, if anything, does it propel? you have notebooks filled with columns of words. they are suffocating you, yet you are always listening for more. you want to be inside the language—you consider how long it would take to write all the words—but you do not want to document as much as you want to do damage to the assumed stability of the document. you are already inside the language, and it is a prison. you mean to escape, to become a kind of trouble. you entered through the broken line of genealogy, but its cracked branches were unable to hold you, so you leapt from the split limbs of that tree onto a moving train, or maybe you are only tricking yourself to believe you were not already aboard it. if the body were a machine, you are unsure how you would name this technology. naming, a practice of enclosure, a way to distinguish and draw a limit. what is the velocity of the train you are writing? train. a name for a type of machinery of mobility but also what kept your maternal grandfather in suspension. you are writing (or is that riding?) the train, which is to say the body, or that the body of your grandfather was sentenced to a kind of automation. what are the proper names of dead things when death is anchored in their ontology (or lack thereof)? what you are trying to ask is how do we name death for those to whom it does not happen? how do we name death for those who are constituted by it? how to not just rename the *Dead Book* in the writing? here logic is limited also, which is why you are writing this until your so-called rational mind tells you it knows no more, and then you will begin. you have yet to begin. you have begun visiting abandoned rail yards, walking along their tracks, lying beside them imagining an oncoming train, trying, in your mind, to map its course. you keep thinking about Henry Dumas, how he boarded that train in 1968, the many fictions that are produced around the encounter he had with a passenger aboard. their supposed argument. an alleged pistol, which was in some accounts a knife, while in others Sun Ra managed to keep Henry from taking any weapon with him. how the transit cop shot him in the chest, perhaps without a second thought. Toni Morrison, who reached into that long hallway to gift us the echo of Henry's writing—later to be an *Echo Tree*—tells you that the circumstances of his death remain unclear. you are unsure what is not clear about the dying. the same dying that Henry would tell us that *the people get tired of*. there is a blur in the accounts, their multiplicity, the standing legitimacy of the transit cop cracking open Henry's chest with their bullet, another kind of collision, another kind of train. you keep thinking of the time between when Henry boards the train and when the bullet breaks Henry's body open as a sentence; you wonder how long this sentence is, you attempt to reconstruct it, rupture it. but Henry is still gone, as is your grandfather, and there are no trains arriving on this abandoned rail yard where you are laying your body now over the tracks, but you feel the precarity, of that sentence, of a bullet, a train, and a black body, or just the banality of labor and time slowly eating away at or transforming that body into a ghost. there is nothing spectacular to see here, just a body lying over ruins. but this is also a presumption that there is a distinction to be made between your body and ruins, that you may differentiate between Henry and the spectacular undoing of his body or your maternal grandfather and the slow decay of his own. or as Stephanie Smallwood writes, *in many slave-holding societies the social death of the slave functioned precisely to empower him to navigate, in his liminality, through be-twixt and between places where full members of society could not.* you understand this liminality, this be-twixt and betweenness, to be a kind of ghostliness. you understand your maternal grandfather and Henry to have been ghosts before the slow and fast collisions that unmade their bodies. you are concerned that you are a ghost as well, that you are not a safe distance from the implication of these conclusions. there is no healing to be found here. no catharsis. the text, not unlike the train, is moving. but in the sleeping car there are those who are not resting, do not sleep, are suspended in exhaustion. maybe you have only ever been attempting to exhaust what is exhausting you. to bring some overdetermined narrative to its limit. *this narrative isn't reliable* says Mirene Arsanios. this reliable narrative—isn't this reliable? this isn't reliable. this isn't narrative—this isn't. you keep reading between and across texts, always looking as though on the other side of a set of tracks, this reading habit built from longing, this urge to weave some cross-stitched book of the dead, and maybe it's just the loneliness making you eager to converse with so many of your unpeopled kin, those you are not materially with. with, as indicating presence. but isn't this the opposite of the ghost? is the ghost not of the order of the absented? of the without. you want ghosts that haunt, that howl, that are not of the silent film. you want ghosts that scream and shake the world of its plastic performances: they did not all live happily ever after, they all after/ed, they not ever, they not. you are reluctant to believe with Smallwood that this spectral space of the below and of excess is a function of power, of the ghost being empowered. not even the ghosts of this story can turn the premature dying into uncountable rays of light or a limitless otherwise. you want to believe there to be something generative in the negation, that through negation, like building a bridge into an abyss, one can roll the dice against the world. you don't like the odds. the wallet already came to you empty. the wallet was likely already mostly empty while it was carried by your maternal grandfather. you are carrying it now, with its compartment for letters and stamps. you are carrying it, reaching into those compartments, into the dense emptiness of their folds and seeing what might be held, what might be possible in the position of the hold, in the suspension that you are here no longer working against but moving toward. you are running toward suspension, a kind of mobile immobility, where you are trying again and again to detonate the margins of those two terms, to undiscipline the borders of what moves or presumably does not as you hurl them into collision. the train wreck mobilizes the theater you are arranging, but the train is a wreck with or without the fantastic crashes of these monumental machines, though you watch these unfold also in report after report. the train is a wreck in that buried beneath that word and aboard that machine is the theft of land, is blood, is terror, is expansion, an expansive hunger without abatement. buried are those who remain without burial, who are now riding some spectral train, its whistle no longer a whistle but a set of knives moving across the air. you are not sure what you want or what you are meaning to say by this, an unconscious desire perhaps to leave meaning behind, to part ways with its expectations, with some belief that the stakes will have been clearly laid out and the objective made clear. you are not aiming at a single point on an object at a designated distance, your aim is everything, and nothing too. you mean to lie. you mean to speculate on your specters, your *Pedagogy of Crossing*, a dream lyric of memories not your own. it is being crafted here. the person who crafted them consorts with ghosts. you've learned to live with ghosts. to ride aboard the spectral train with splintered time. you've heard recurrence, something lingering between time. you've been gone, you've not been here. here you've mourned, you've been the sadness and the specter, swallowed a rail yard and spit out its bones, you've been alone, lonely, inheriting holes, nothing whole, you've been working your way into the hold, the abyssal, been strange, deranged, a changeling left out in the night, nothing recovered, you've been without cover, no sanctuary, wrecked and the wreckage, a part of some ongoing collision with a world that finds its gears in your undoing, you've been unsure of what you're doing, you've been doing it still, no feat of will, something mad in your composition, you've been attempting to exhaust composition, to make the text decompose, to make of this body a ghost, you mean to be the haunting, you've been the howl, and here, not in this place, in this position, you are at a limit, here in this position you are at the edge of your knowing, wanting to look over, to climb through the torn borders of your abbreviated documents, the terminal wreckage of them, and with their frayed edges rewrite all our names . . .

rewrite all our names...
rewrite all our names...
rewrite all our names...
rewrite all our names...

rewrite all our names...
rewrite all our names...

Notes and Permission Acknowledgments

FOREWORD

I start in the middle . . . at once: John Coltrane. Licensed courtesy of Jowcol Music.

texture of sound . . . overcome with Spirit: Ashon T. Crawley, *Blackpentecostal Breath: The Aesthetics of Possibility* (Fordham University Press, 2017), 45.

swallowed up in chaos, . . . darkness does not present a point of departure, contains no beginning, . . . and no end, see through the morning wall [and] tear the thousand gray veils of the sky away: James Baldwin, *Go Tell It on the Mountain* (Vintage International, 2013), 196, 221.

These sentences will gather . . . in equation: Renee Gladman, *Plans for Sentences* (Wave Books, 2022), 21.

COMPORT(ER)

How does one narrate . . . loss: Frank B. Wilderson III, *Afropessimism* (Liveright, 2020), 16. Reprinted with permission.

They will say that I . . . small cells: Dawn Lundy Martin, *Life in a Box Is a Pretty Life* (Nightboat Books, 2017), 78. Reprinted with permission.

For background on John Henry, I consulted Scott Reynolds Nelson's *Steel Drivin' Man: John Henry, the Untold Story of an American Legend* (Oxford University Press, 2006). Nelson lays out the historical existence of John Henry—long understood as a legend—who was a nineteen-year-old arrested for theft and put to work on the C&O railroad. May his stolen life be honored.

loophole of retreat: See Harriet Jacobs, *Incidents in the Life of a Slave Girl: An Autobiographical Account of an Escaped Slave and Abolitionist* [1861] (Skyhorse, 2015), 81.

For the etymology of zero, see *Online Etymology Dictionary*, www.etymonline.com/search?q=zero.

For background on Henry Box Brown, I consulted *Narrative of the Life of Henry Box Brown* (Oxford University Press, 2003), xi.

three hundred black migrants . . . contrabands of war: See Abram L. Harris, "The Negro Population in Minneapolis: A Study of Race Relations," in *Race, Radicalism, and Reform* (Routledge, 1989), 64–99. https://doi.org/10.4324/9781351317443-8.

the term *free black* carries tension . . . ontological catastrophe: See Calvin L. Warren, *Ontological Terror: Blackness, Nihilism, and Emancipation* (Duke University Press, 2018), 15.

SENTENCED

Is there an underground . . . sentence: Fred Moten, afterword to Renee Gladman, *Prose Architectures* (Wave Books, 2017), 112. Reprinted with permission.

A note on form. "Sentenced" borrows its form from the looping sentence that is the first poem in Anthony Cody's *Borderland Apocrypha* (Omnidawn, 2020).

In 1903 Charles F. Anderson wrote a widely circulated letter that would later become the pamphlet "Freeman Yet Slaves Under 'Abe' Lincoln's Son or Service and Wages of Pullman Porters" where he details the terrible working conditions of porters, linking them to slavery, and notably identifies how porters would be so exhausted from the labor that it was common for a number of them to just drop dead. This is one plausible understanding of the cause for the death of my great grandfather. For more on Charles Anderson and his pamphlet, see Blair LM Kelley, *Black Folk: The Roots of the Black Working Class* (Liveright, 2023).

Image of "St. Paul Man Dies After Illness of Short Duration" from *St. Paul Recorder* reproduced with the permission of *The Minnesota Spokesman-Recorder*.

continues to produce [your] fast and slow death: See Christina Sharpe, *In the Wake: On Blackness and Being* (Duke University Press, 2016), 116.

changing same: See Nathaniel Mackey, "The Changing Same: Black Music in the Poetry of Amiri Baraka," *boundary* 2, vol. 6, no. 2 (winter 1978).

LOOK WHERE IT AIN'T

You have to look where it ain't: Kentifrican proverb, "Artist Talk: Kenyatta A. C. Hinkle: Navigating Ain'tness: Exploring the Kentifrica Archive," Art + Practice, 2015. https://artandpractice.org/public-programs/program/artist-talk-kenyatta-a-c-hinkle-navigating-aintness-exploring-the-kentifrica-archive/. Reprinted with permission.

in the beginning . . . an' black ain't: See Ralph Ellison, *Invisible Man* (Vintage International, 1995), 9.

a photograph is like a poem . . . the limit: See Monica Huerta, *Magical Habits* (Duke University Press, 2021), 85.

ON TONGUES

I think I am possessed by . . . her mother's: Moon Charania, "Prologue," in *Archive of Tongues: An Intimate History of Brownness* (Duke University Press, 2023), xxi. Copyright 2023 by Duke University Press. All rights reserved. Republished by permission of the copyright holder and the Publisher. www.dukeupress.edu.

. . . that's all them . . . words: Derek Walcott, "The Schooner Flight" in *The Star-Apple Kingdom* (Farrar, Straus and Giroux, 1979).

nonsense is . . . fugitive presence: Fred Moten, *Stolen Life* (Duke University Press, 2018), 1.

For more on the **aesthetic practice** as opposed to the doxological see Ashon T. Crawley, *Blackpentecostal Breath: The Aesthetics of Possibility* (Fordham University Press, 2017), 4.

about to disappear: See Saidiya Hartman where she notes how "to read the archive is to enter a mortuary; it permits one final viewing and allows for a last glimpse at persons about to disappear into the slave hold," in *Lose Your Mother: A Journey Along the Atlantic Slave Route* (Farrar, Straus and Giroux, 2008), 17.

dance . . . is only realized at the moment of its disappearance is a description Dr. Ananya Chatterjea made of dance and its not being a medium in which an art object is produced, at the onset of a movement class called Just Craft.

ALICE

oh you wanna strip away . . . don't waste your candor on bystanders: See "Bystanders (in space)," track 11 on Moses Sumney, *Live from Blackalachia*, Tuntum, 2021.

FOOT NOTES

We do not ride on the railroad; it rides upon us: Henry David Thoreau, *Walden or, Life in the Woods* (MVP, 2023), 45, Kindle.

For background on Henry Dumas, I consulted Jeffrey B. Leak's *Visible Man: The Life of Henry Dumas* (University of Georgia Press, 2014).

genius, an absolute genius . . . the mess: See Toni Morrison, "On Behalf of Henry Dumas," *Black American Literature Forum*, vol. 22, no. 2 (1988), 310.

the people get tired of dying: See Henry Dumas, *Echo Tree* (Coffee House Press, 2021), 377.

volatile . . . impossible: See Saidiya Hartman, "Venus in Two Acts," *Small Axe: A Caribbean Journal of Criticism*, vol. 12, no. 2 (2008), 1–14.

THE BLACK HISTORICAL IS ALREADY THE HAUNTOLOGICAL

we are all haunted . . . never found rest . . .: fahima ife, "Maroon Choreography," in *Maroon Choreography* (Duke University Press, 2021), 78–91.

representation of language free from lexical and syntactic limits: See Caroline Kent's description of the installation *How Objects Move Through Walls* (Company Projects, 2018).

in many slaveholding societies . . . could not: See Stephanie E. Smallwood, *Saltwater Slavery: A Middle Passage from Africa to American Diaspora* (Harvard University Press, 2008), 59.

this narrative isn't reliable: See Mirene Arsanios, *The Autobiography of a Language* (Futurepoem, 2022), 2.

Images on pages 16, 19, 20, 35, 37, 181: Courtesy of the National Archives in Atlanta.

Always Acknowledgment

writing *Without Terminus* was among the most difficult things i've ever taken on. at first i thought that this would be a tightly woven historical record of railroad companies, labor unions, and the failure of the overdetermined uplift narrative to see porters like my grandfather. and some of that is retained, but it quickly became more and more unwieldy, a record more about loss, and what is beyond retrieval or repair. it required that i speak with ghosts against any belief in the possibility of a response, which in part might just be what it means to work with the black historical record. the black historical is already the hauntological. i could not have done this without the questions and prompting and support of so many. thank you to Kao Kalia Yang, for your class Women Writing War, for your pedagogical acumen, your close listening, and your encouragement in the early stages of my writing *Without Terminus*. thank you to Douglas Kearney, adviser, friend, and standard bearer, you have seen every iteration of this book and asked the most pressing questions, offered the most precious insights. years ago now i remember you being in conversation with Evie Shockley and as an aside discussing black writerly attempts at haunting our own memories. that's all i'm trying to do here in this work. special thanks to Dr. Aaron Mallory; your friendship and almost daily conversations on blackness and loss, and what cannot be recovered but that we stubbornly keep trying to recover, were instrumental. many thanks to Dr. Megan Finch for helping me think through blackness, madness, and constraints. to Phillip Metres for the courage to not let go of tenderness, to Anni Liu and Brittany Torres Rivera for your careful editorial reading and Carmen Giménez for your belief in this work and giving it a home at Graywolf. Steven Dunn, Rion Almicar Scott, Said Shaiye, Ron Austin, and Donald Quist, our thread kept me level. Jimmy Patiño, Jose Luis Villasenor, Filiberto Nolasco Gomez, Jermaine Ross, Aaron Mallory, and Vichet Chhuon, love ya'll. Dr. Kathryn Nuerenberger, Krys Belc, Amalia Tenuta,

Kachina Yeager, Sarah Haas, Talia Webster, and Verna Wong and so many others who endured my endless trains of thought, thank you for your patience and close reading. many thanks to *Obsidian*, *Brink*, *Ploughshares*, *Angel City Review*, and the Academy of American Poets for publishing earlier versions of selected work. and the thanks could go on, always acknowledgment. and i write these words amid ongoing genocides emerging from a world built on dispossession, and the language is limited as are the attempts to go beyond it. i do not consent to these words, these words are all i have. always acknowledgment. the shortcomings are mine alone.

chaun webster is a poet and graphic designer whose work contends with the spatial, temporal, and interpretive limitations of writing to represent blackness outside of regimes of death and dying. webster's work has appeared in numerous journals including *Obsidian*, the Academy of American Poets' Poem-a-Day, *The Rumpus*, *Angel City Review*, *Tilted House*, and *Social Text*. webster is the author of *Gentry!fication: or the scene of the crime* (Noemi Press) and *Wail Song: wading in the water at the end of the world* (Black Ocean). Both books received the Minnesota Book Award for poetry. *Without Terminus* is his first work of nonfiction.

Graywolf Press publishes risk-taking, visionary writers who transform culture through literature. As a nonprofit organization, Graywolf relies on the generous support of its donors to bring books like this one into the world.

This publication is made possible, in part, by the voters of Minnesota through a Minnesota State Arts Board Operating Support grant, thanks to a legislative appropriation from the arts and cultural heritage fund. Significant support has also been provided by other generous contributions from foundations, corporations, and individuals. To these supporters we offer our heartfelt thanks.

To learn more about Graywolf's books
and authors or make a tax-deductible donation,
please visit www.graywolfpress.org.

The text of *Without Terminus* is set in Baskerville.
Book design by chaun webster.
Composition by Bookmobile Design & Digital
Publisher Services, Minneapolis, Minnesota.
Manufactured by Versa Press on acid-free,
30 percent postconsumer wastepaper.